Diagonal (or On-Point) Set

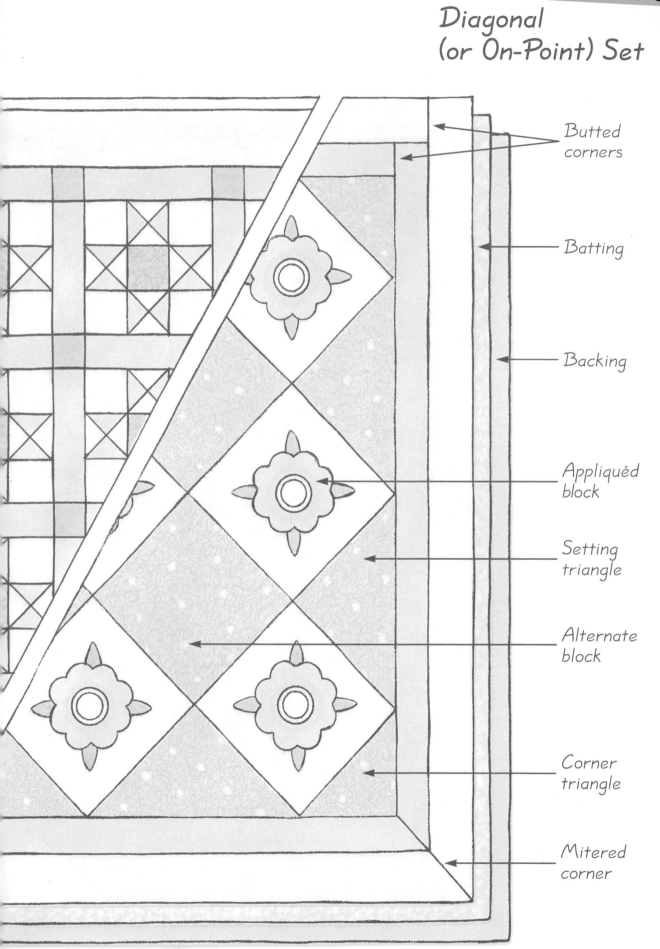

Butted corners

Batting

Backing

Appliquéd block

Setting triangle

Alternate block

Corner triangle

Mitered corner

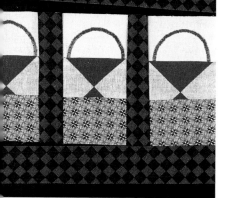
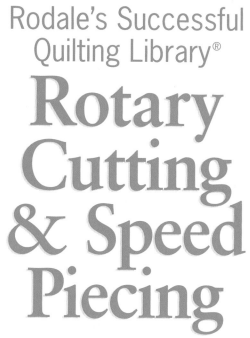

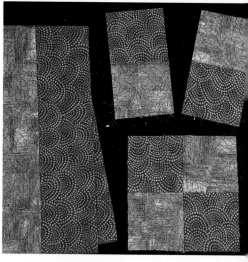

Rodale's Successful
Quilting Library®

Rotary
Cutting
& Speed
Piecing

Sarah Sacks Dunn
Editor

RODALE®

RODALE

WE INSPIRE AND ENABLE PEOPLE TO IMPROVE
THEIR LIVES AND THE WORLD AROUND THEM

We're always happy to hear from you.

For questions or comments concerning
the editorial content of this book,
please write to:

Rodale Book Readers' Service
33 East Minor Street
Emmaus, PA 18098

Look for other Rodale books
wherever books are sold. Or call us at
(800) 848-4735.

For more information about Rodale and
the books and magazines we publish,
visit our World Wide Web site at:
www.rodale.com

On the cover: detail, Old Growth by
Dixie Haywood
On these pages: Woven in Red by Susan Stein
On the following pages: The Fire Inside by
Diane Rode Schneck

Book Producer: Eleanor Levie,
Craft Services, LLC
Art Director: Lisa J. F. Palmer
Editor: Sarah Sacks Dunn
Contributing Editor: Karen Costello Soltys
Writers: Janet Armstrong-Wickell,
Barbara J. Eikmeier, Jane Hall,
Dixie Haywood, Diane Rode Schneck,
Susan Stein, Beth Wheeler, and
Darra Duffy Williamson
Photographer: John P. Hamel
Illustrator: Mario Ferro
Models: Erana Bumbardatore,
Colleen Kennedy-Morgan,
Coline Nitzsche-Eberling
Copy Editors: Nancy N. Bailey and
Erana Bumbardatore
Indexer: Nan N. Badgett

Rodale Inc.
Editorial Manager, Quilt Continuity:
Ellen Pahl
Studio Manager: Leslie M. Keefe
Manufacturing Manager: Mark Krahforst
Manufacturing Coordinator: Patrick T. Smith
Photography Editor: James A. Gallucci
Series Designer: Sue Gettlin

**Library of Congress Cataloging-in-
Publication Data**

Rotary cutting & speed piecing / Sarah S.
Dunn, editor.
p. cm. — (Rodale's successful
quilting library)
Includes index.
ISBN 1–57954–192–5 (hardcover)
1. Quilting. 2. Patchwork. I. Dunn,
Sarah S. II. Series.
TT835.R637 2000
746.46—dc21 99–087180

Distributed in the book trade
by St. Martin's Press

2 4 6 8 10 9 7 5 3 1 hardcover

Contents

Introduction

When I first began to quilt, I had one placid son, a job with regular hours, and a spare bedroom on the second floor. I quilted at will, designed gift quilts, took quilting classes, and made a quilt for my son's bed. Now several years, another child, and a freelance career later, my sewing room has been demoted from an upstairs bedroom to a nook in the kitchen (see page 13). When I do find time to quilt, it's usually last minute—a quick gift for a special friend, teacher, or relative.

So how do I do it? Well, I look for shortcuts, speedy techniques, and other ways to shorten the time I spend but still enable me to make a quilt I'm proud of; one that I want people to know I made. I rarely do anything by hand: I rely heavily on my rotary cutter and my trusty sewing machine. And I learned very early that to do it right the first time (even if it takes a little longer) is to save time in the long run.

That's why this book was a thrill for me to work on. Every technique is one that I can guarantee will produce great results with a minimum of time and frustration. Need a quick wedding quilt? Try one of the tips in "Speedy BIG Quilts" on page 108. Need ideas for strip-pieced blocks? See "Build Your Strip-Piecing Skills" on page 32. And you'll learn about triangle squares, string piecing, and loads of other amazing little techniques that you can use to make a stunner of a quilt in an incredibly short amount of time. And be sure to read "20 Top Tips for Rotary Cutting" on page 8 to make sure that you use and maintain your equipment properly.

While I still take time when I can to make those special heirloom quilts for my kids, rotary cutting and speed piecing ensure that I'll finish these projects before they reach adulthood. I also turn to speedy techniques to lavish a little extra attention on pieced backings that are worthy of the quilt tops. I'm currently working on a pastel strip-pieced design to back an antique reproduction quilt for my daughter. Since it's a lot less labor-intensive and the fabrics are more replaceable, I'll be spreading out this reverse side—at least until she's outgrown jumping on the bed.

The ideas for this book are basic ones, taken to a higher level by strip piecing and the rotary cutter, that indispensable tool we all know and love. We called on experts who wield a rotary cutter like no others—Barb Eikmeier, Jane Hall, Dixie Haywood, Diane Rode Schneck, Susan Stein, Beth Wheeler, Janet Wickell, and Darra Duffy Williamson all shared their wisdom, tips, and favorite techniques for clever ways to speed up quilting using speedy cutting and piecing combinations. Then, based on their instructions, detailed samples were sewn for the photographs so you could see, step-by-step, ways to make your quilting quicker, more efficient, and more accurate the first time.

What's the upshot of all this? For one thing, less guilt and more quilting time! For instance, when a friend oohs and aahs over the quilt I made for my cousin's baby and begs me to make one for her grandchild-to-be, I used to say, "Sorry, I don't have time." Now, I can avoid the guilt of saying no by pulling out this book, picking a quick technique, and getting out my cutting equipment—and also letting her help! The best part of this book for me was remembering that quilting is more fun with a buddy, as the final chapter (see page 114) explains.

So read through the chapters as fast as you can . . . then head for your sewing room (or space or corner) and get going! You can make a quilt in a weekend that you'll be just as proud of as one that took a month or more—it's all in your attitude (and in your rotary cutter)!

Sarah Sacks Dunn

Sarah Sacks Dunn
Editor

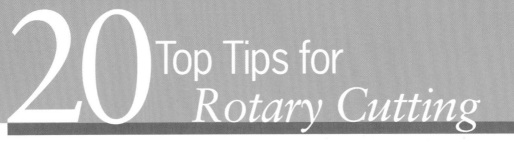
1 Always use a clean, sharp blade in your rotary cutter. Dull blades aren't as accurate, and they are more likely to skip threads and force you to recut your fabric. Plus, exerting the extra pressure to compensate for a dull blade is hard on your hand and wrist. A dull blade can be more dangerous, too; as you push harder, you may push the blade up over the ruler, cutting a finger.

2 Always cut away from yourself. Not only does it make for a more accurate cut because you get a better view of your fabric and ruler's edge, but it also prevents you from getting hurt.

3 Always close the blade guard on your rotary cutter when you are not actively cutting fabric. Any quilter will tell you that just the slightest bump into an open blade is very painful. Not to mention, you don't want bloodstains on your fabric.

4 Hold the handle of your rotary cutter at about a 45 degree angle to your cutting surface. Keep the blade perfectly perpendicular (straight up and down) to the cutting surface, and butted up against the edge of a thick acrylic rotary ruler. You'll be able to exert the necessary pressure, and you'll get a straighter cut.

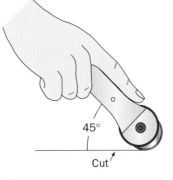

5 Use the same brand of ruler throughout your project, and try to use the same lighting and surface setup each time as well. Shadows from different rulers, discrepancies in ruler manufacture, brightness variations in your cutting area, and varying height of your cutting surface can all make small differences in the way you cut. And while a $1/16$-inch difference may not be much in an individual patch, it adds up across the width of a quilt made of a few dozen patches.

6 Never cut over pins or anything other than fabric. This can cause nicks in your blade. Worse, it can cause the cutter to jump and cause nicks in your hand.

7 Place your cutting mat on a firm, flat surface. Always cut on a mat specially designed for rotary cutting. Other surfaces will dull the blade and will not provide adequate protection to the surface beneath. Also, some surfaces may not "absorb" the blade, and the cutter can skip or bounce, producing mistakes or injuries.

8 Keep your rotary cutter clean and in good working condition. Between blade changes, remove the blade and wipe off all lint and dust. Inspect the blade for nicks and the parts for wear; both can make cutting more difficult. Replace your blade as soon as you notice any nicks; a sure sign of this is when your cutter skips threads as you're cutting.

9 Many quilters find it is easier to cut while standing. This reduces the amount of pressure you have to put on the cutter, gives you a better view of what you're cutting, and enables you to have a longer reach and, therefore, a cleaner cut.

10 Keep your cutting mat in good condition. Store it flat, if possible, and away from heat and sunlight. A warped mat is dangerous and inaccurate to cut on. If you don't have flat storage, try this: Hang your mat from a skirt or pants hanger in your closet.

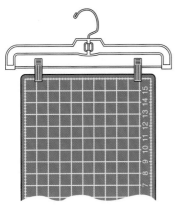

11 Cutters come in different sizes for good reasons. A cutter with a small (28mm diameter) blade is good for cutting around curves and around templates. A medium-size (45mm) blade is good for general-purpose cutting of up to four layers of fabric. If you're cutting through many layers or a particularly troublesome fabric (such as a woven or stiff fabric), use a larger (60mm) cutter. Be conservative about the number of layers you cut. Fewer layers make for greater accuracy. Always check the packaging for the manufacturer's guidelines for your particular rotary cutter.

12 When you change the blade on your rotary cutter, throw the old one away safely. Either place it in the plastic case the new blade came in or cover it in some other fashion so no one gets cut accidentally. Wrap a few layers of wide, ribbed strapping tape

around your old blade, or tape it inside a folded index card.

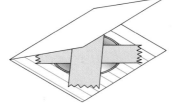

13 Always make sure your fingers (and anyone else's!) are away from the edge of your ruler as you cut.

14 Many mats are reversible, with a lighter color on one side and a darker color on the other. If your fabric blends in too much with the color on one side, flip the mat over for higher contrast and better cutting accuracy.

15 Buy the largest mat your cutting area will accommodate. The extra size comes in handy for manipulating large yardages and cutting long borders.

16 When cutting strips for long strip sets, cut along the lengthwise grain whenever possible. The threads along the length of fabric yardage have very little stretch, so the sewn strips are much less likely to become misshapen. Be sure to remove the selvages (the very tightly woven edges).

Selvages

17 If you're working with two fabrics that will eventually be sewn together, iron them together with right sides facing. Then they are perfectly aligned, slightly "stuck" together from the pressing, and ready to sew—with or without pinning. This technique is especially useful when you're strip piecing and making half-square triangles.

18 When you are transporting your rotary cutter, be doubly safe about protecting it and you! Not only should you raise the blade guard, but you should also encase the cutter in sturdy packaging. Use an eyeglass case, make a felt bag, or purchase a rotary blade cover from your local quilt shop or mail-order source.

19 When cutting woven plaids or checks, let the lines in the fabric guide alignment. Coax the threads to lie straight under your ruler, and keep pressure on your ruler exactly where your cutter is slicing through the fabric.

20 When you start feeling tired, stop cutting! The probability of inaccuracy and injury increases dramatically when you're fatigued.

Streamline
Your Workspace

A corner to cut, a spot to stitch, a place to press . . . Let's face it: The quiltmaking process can consume lots of space! And when the need for elbow room is coupled with the need to store fabric, thread, batting, and notions, the result might easily become a logistical nightmare. Our solution? A collection of creative ideas and tips to help you make the most of your space, whether you have a private studio devoted entirely to quiltmaking or a corner carved from a busy room in your house.

Getting Ready

Approach the organization—or reorganization—of your quilting space much as you would any other home improvement project. Begin by assessing your specific cutting and sewing practices.

• Must you dismantle your work area regularly to free space for mealtime, homework, or houseguests? If so, you'll need convenient and ample storage for even the most basic equipment, such as your iron and sewing machine.

• Do you prefer sitting or standing as you cut and press? How tall are you? Are you right-handed? left-handed? physically challenged? Do inquisitive little fingers have access to your work area? Each of these factors will ultimately affect the arrangement of your sewing area—the height of cutting and sewing surfaces, placement of ironing stations and cutting boards, location of storage, and so on.

• Are you a daytime stitcher who needs natural light, or are you a night owl who depends on artificial lighting?

• Is your "technology" state of the art? Sewing machines, computers, sergers, and irons all require electricity. You'll need lots of conveniently located outlets and a reliable power source.

• Inventory your fabric, notions, and equipment to determine how much and what type of storage you'll need. Do you buy fabric by the fat quarter, the yard, or the bolt? Save scraps? Collect books, magazines, and gadgets?

Once you've considered your particular needs and preferences, you are ready to evaluate the space at hand and to create a comfortable, efficient work area tailor-made for you!

A Room of Your Own

Customize a Studio

When you have a room to use just for a sewing space, make the most of every inch. This dream space belongs to Judy Roche, an antique quilt collector who loves making reproduction and contemporary quilts. **Judy's space uses a T-formation, with sketching, planning, and pressing areas at the top of the T, and a sewing area along its stem. A small cutting mat is handy by her machine and a separate, full-size cutting table is nearby.** This is especially efficient for large projects that use speedy rotary cutting techniques.

A Little Library

Tip

Utilize your space from floor to ceiling. Mount bookshelves over doors and windows; use grid systems or corkboard to keep supplies within reach.

Are you a collector of quilting books and magazines? **Judy had a wall of bookshelves built to hold her sources of ideas and information.** And with all the quilting shows these days, a TV provides information and inspiration as well as entertainment when completing some of the more mundane quilting tasks.

Design Wall Deluxe

Tip

When you go to the lumberyard, take your pins and try pushing them into the surface of materials you're auditioning for a design wall.

Trying out combinations of colors, shapes, and sizes as well as blocks, settings, and borders is so much easier with a design wall. **Judy's design wall is small but covers an entire wall area, where ½-inch-thick sheets of fiberboard are permanently affixed with screws.** Look for wallboard, Homosote, or any soft but dense, durable material sold in 4 × 8-foot sheets at the lumberyard. You will be able to arrange and rearrange patches, units, and quilt blocks, using pins to keep pieces in place.

Material-ism on View

Tip

Spend precious time sewing, not searching! Label all opaque containers and boxes so the contents are obvious at a glance.

Fabric storage is always a challenge. **Sort fabric in any way that makes sense to you: by size (yard, ½ yard, etc.), by color, by value, or by the type of print (florals, geometrics, etc.).** Ideally, you'll want fabric easy to see and neatly stacked, as Judy has done on her built-in shelves. If space is at a premium in your sewing room, steal it wherever you can—a nearby linen or hall closet, bureau drawers, cabinets, and even ventilated boxes kept under a bed.

The Kitchen Quilter

When what you have to work with is a corner of a room, make the most of the space you have available to you. Editor Sarah Dunn does all her quilting in her kitchen, and she uses every spare square inch between the refrigerator and the kitchen shelving!

• With the help of magnets, the side of the refrigerator doubles as a makeshift design wall, keeping sample blocks and sketches of designs within sight. There are also "quilting" magnets available, cut into standard patch shapes, to help you design quilt blocks. (Check for these in your local quilt shop or favorite mail-order catalog.) Or use children's magnetic shapes to play with arrangements.

• The windowsill is the perfect place to store large rulers where they're accessible but not in the way. And because they're clear plastic, they still let in natural light.

• A sturdy table holds the sewing machine, pins, and a small cutting mat and ruler. A decorative basket doubles as a place to store thread and other small notions attractively and efficiently.

• A small supplies and notions cabinet fits neatly underneath the sewing table, out of the way of kitchen traffic. Locking drawers keep sharp cutters, pins, and scissors out of the hands of small children. A place for hanging files in the top section keeps patterns, templates, magazines and drafting supplies handy.

• A former microwave cart holds fabrics and supplies on its shelves and in its drawer, while the top doubles as a sturdy cutting or pressing surface. Lock the wheels in place—or remove them—so the cart stays put for rotary cutting. The Brooklyn Revolver shown on top of the cart (see "Resources" on page 125) is a handy revolving cutting surface, eliminating the need to move around while cutting and making for an even more efficient work space.

• The kitchen island is the perfect surface for a larger cutting/pressing station. It's well lit, has an outlet nearby, and is just the right height for lengthy sessions of cutting yardage, pressing seams, or layering and basting.

STREAMLINE YOUR WORKSPACE

A Transformed Guest Room

Multipurpose to the Max

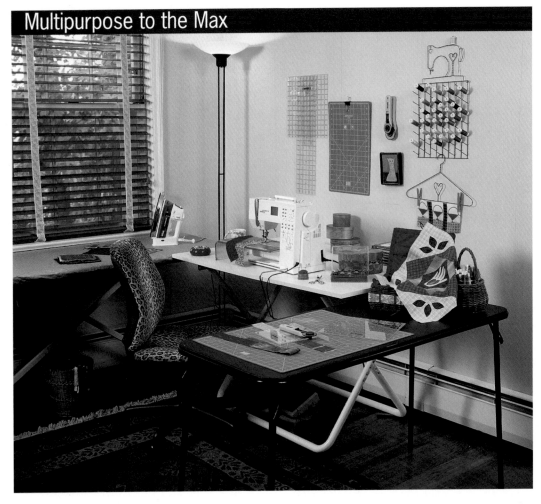

When your quilting space doubles as a guest room, it's time to get creative with quick and easy ways to make your guests feel as if the room exists just for them. Likewise, when they go home, you want to be able to get back in your sewing seat without having to rearrange all the furniture.

This U-shaped arrangement of cutting, sewing, and pressing areas occupies a corner of book producer Eleanor Levie's guest room. The layout ensures that her quilting activities can speed along without her constantly having to get up and down.

An ironing board can serve as one leg of your U-shaped workstation. Adjust the board's height so that it is even with your sewing surface. A sturdy folding table is the second leg of the U. This handy cutting station is just the ticket when you're doing combination techniques such as strip piecing. Cut the strips at this leg of the U, turn to the base of the U to sew them to-

gether, press them on the opposite leg of the U, then return to the cutting table to cut segments from your strip set. You'll turn from cutting to stitching to pressing—and back again—without ever having to leave your chair.

The window to the left lets in natural light, and the wood blinds give privacy to your guests during their stay. A corner torchiere lamp adds light to all three areas and illuminates the rest of the room as well.

Eleanor chose decorative hangers and racks to hold and display her colorful threads and blocks on the wall. Pretty baskets, decoupage boxes, and other attractive containers hold her notions and equipment, making the space homey as well as useful. In addition, the table and ironing board fold up quickly and store flat, enabling her to hide the evidence of the messiest work-in-progress. When out-of-towners visit, they'll feel pampered and comfortable!

Concealed Work-in-Progress

This quilt cleverly hides a large design wall—without disturbing your design deliberations. When you want to use the design wall, just pull the quilt to one side, or take it down altogether. Seek out versatile hardware for hanging the quilt, so that you can put it up and take it down with ease. Several wood quilt clips hold this patchwork classic in place, but you can also order special display moldings that clamp the top edge of a quilt in place but allow for easy removal. Try to place clips or clamps every 10 inches or so to distribute the weight of the quilt evenly across the top and thereby lessen the stress on the fibers.

See "Resources" on page 125 for the Display-away, and check out quilt shops and quilter's catalogs for other mounting apparatus.

Closet of Conveniences

Store the supplies and fabrics you aren't currently using efficiently and attractively in part of your guest closet. **Shelving for fabrics, cabinets for papers and patterns, and containers for notions and supplies can all be kept in a modest-size closet, without intruding on your guests' space.** If you install a good light, you can even use a closet as a workstation.

May the Seat Be Comfortable!

An adjustable, swivel-style office chair with wheels is a most important element for any sewing space. You can raise and lower the seat for maximum support during marathon stretches at the sewing machine as well as maneuver effortlessly from cutting to pressing and back again. An ergonomic design and adjustable arms can both further increase your comfort level.

A pillow or foam form to support your lower back may turn a so-so seat into a treat to work from.

STREAMLINE YOUR WORKSPACE

Accuracy
Guaranteed

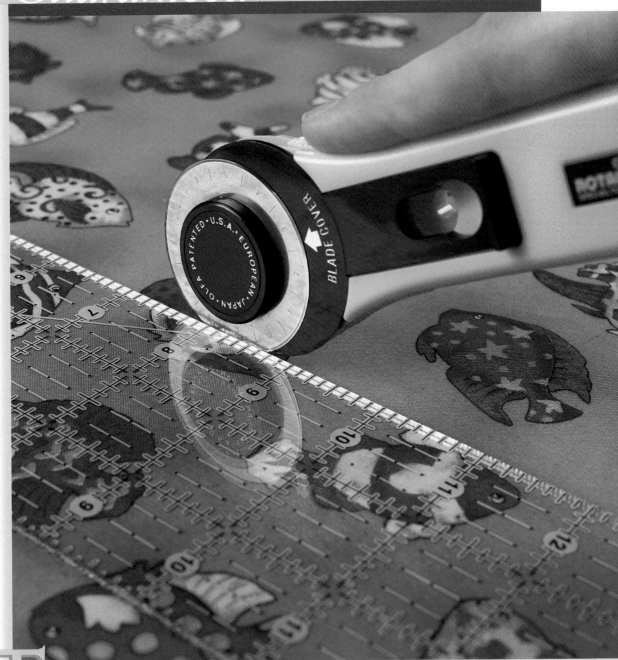

There is little doubt: The quilt world has been revolutionized by the introduction and rousing popularity of the rotary cutter. This timesaving gadget enables us to produce more quilts than ever before and to make them more quickly and efficiently than ever. As with any tool, you must prepare your fabric carefully to take advantage of all that the rotary cutter offers you. These tips will help ensure that you get the most accuracy from your invaluable rotary cutter.

Getting Ready

The quilting marketplace overflows with rotary cutters, mats, and rulers of every conceivable size, shape, and ergonomic configuration. The tools you select, and how you maintain them, will dramatically affect your success with—and enjoyment of—rotary-cutting techniques. Experiment to find the tools that suit you best.

Focus on quality. As in any other consumer market, you get what you pay for! Sturdy, accurate, user-friendly equipment should feel comfortable when you handle it and should include directions for use; this will enhance accuracy from the start.

Care for your tools. Clean and oil your rotary cutter regularly, and keep the blade sharp. Avoid metal or metal-edged wooden rulers that can damage the blades . . . and never run over pins! To prevent warping, store cutting mats and rulers flat and away from heat.

What You'll Need

- **100% cotton fabric, prewashed**
- **Iron and ironing surface**
- **Spray starch**
- **Rotary cutter**
- **Replacement blades or rotary-blade sharpener**
- **Self-healing cutting mat**
- **Acrylic gridded rulers in a variety of sizes**
- **Adhesive sandpaper patches or strips**
- **Suctioned handles for use with rotary rulers (optional)**

On Your Way to Accurate Cutting

Well Pressed

Carefully pressing your fabric minimizes the possibility of distorted or misshapen strips and pieces, so press your fabric well before you make the very first cut! **Set your iron to the Cotton setting (no steam, please!), then unfold and press the entire piece of fabric.** Press firmly enough to smooth the wrinkles and flatten the center fold, but not so vigorously that you stretch the fabric out of shape. Add a touch of spray starch for a crisp, easy-to-cut finish.

Tip

For greater cutting accuracy, divide an oversize length of fabric into smaller, more manageable pieces before pressing and cutting.

ACCURACY GUARANTEED

Fold, Fold Again

Fold the fabric in half, matching the selvage (lengthwise) edges. **Use the woven selvage to align the fabric since the raw crosswise edge may be frayed or unevenly cut.** Carefully smooth the fabric so that it is free of wrinkles and puckers along this newly folded edge. For greatest accuracy, make only one fold, and cut through just two layers of fabric.

Some quilters double the fabric again so they can make shorter cuts. **To do this, carefully match the folded edge with the selvages.** Smooth any gaps or wrinkles before cutting. With four layers of fabric, the risk of slip page and miscut pieces is greater.

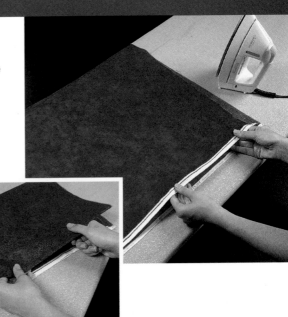

A Perfect Setup

Carefully transfer the pressed and folded fabric to your cutting mat. Place the folded edge of the fabric nearest to you, and—if the mat is gridded—**align this folded edge with a horizontal grid line on the mat.** If you are right-handed, position the bulk of the fabric to your left; if you are left-handed, the bulk of the fabric should be to your right.

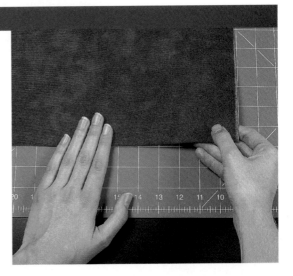

The Cutting Edge

Before cutting your first strip, straighten the raw edge of the pressed and folded fabric. (*Note:* If you are right-handed, you will be trimming the right edge; if you are left-handed, you will be trimming the left.) Align a horizontal line on the ruler precisely with the folded edge of the fabric, making sure the raw edges of the fabric extend beyond the edge of the ruler. **Trim away this narrow strip, and you are assured a clean, straight edge from which to measure and cut.**

Right-handed

Left-handed

Brand Loyalty

It is simply a fact of quilting life that despite today's advanced technology and attention to quality control, all rulers are *not* created equal! The processes involved in mass production result in occasional variations—however slight—from one brand of ruler to the next, or sometimes even within the same brand. For this reason, it is wise to **use the same rotary ruler throughout an entire quilting project.** Those slight variations will be consistent throughout your project, and your patches, units, and blocks will still fit together nicely!

Get a Grip

Accuracy demands that both ruler and fabric remain secure as you rotary cut. Here are solutions for even less-than-steady hands. **Look for a rotary ruler with a raised grid, which when placed "rough" side down, grips the fabric to minimize slippage.** Or, create your own gripping ruler by **attaching sandpaper strips or dots to the underside of your ruler.** Check your quilt shop for precut adhesive patches, or use sandpaper and glue to create your own. **Suctioned gripping handles, which can make it easier to hold the ruler steady,** are also available from quilt shops and via mail order.

Tip

Another no-slip method: Place dots of rubber cement on the underside of your ruler. When they dry, they'll act as nonskid grippers.

Measuring Up to Perfection

You'll maintain accuracy throughout the rotary-cutting and speed-piecing process if you "measure and straighten" as you go. **Double-check and adjust key measurements at each pivotal step: after the initial strips and shapes are cut; after strip sets and block units are pieced; as units are assembled; and when the block is complete.** If necessary, use your rotary cutter and acrylic ruler to trim your unit or block to the correct size. (Don't forget to allow for seam allowances!)

Tip

For extra insurance, periodically realign and restraighten the cut edge of the fabric when rotary cutting a large number of strips.

ACCURACY GUARANTEED

Rotary Cutting
Unusual Shapes

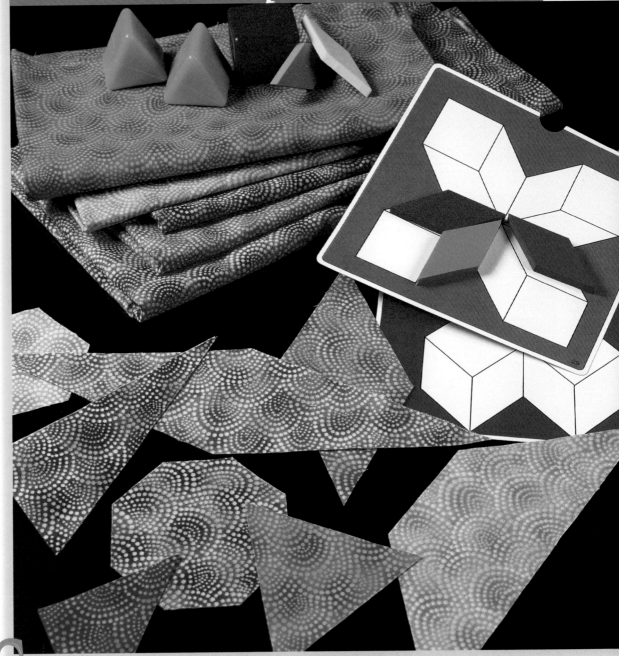

*S*ay good-bye to cumbersome templates, marking tools, and scissors! Rotary-cutting equipment has opened up a whole new world of cutting patches for your quilts—and not just simple squares, rectangles, and triangles. You'll be amazed how quick, easy, and accurate it can be, even when cutting less common shapes. And the best news is that you'll get to the real fun of piecing your quilt in no time.

Getting Ready

The starting point for each shape in this chapter is a strip of fabric (called a "parent" strip) that is cut along the straight grain. The width of the parent strip depends on the finished size of the shape you wish to cut: Instructions for calculating the strip width for each shape are included in the margin tips and in the numbered steps for the shape. If you are left-handed, the cuts you make and the angled lines you use will be mirror images of the ones shown. If your ruler does not have angle lines printed in both directions, you may need to use different ruler positions than those shown. If rotary cutting is new to you, be sure to read "Accuracy Guaranteed," starting on page 16, before beginning.

What You'll Need

Fabric, prewashed and pressed

Rotary cutter and mat

Acrylic ruler with 30, 45, and 60 degree angle lines

Marking pencil

Equilateral Triangle

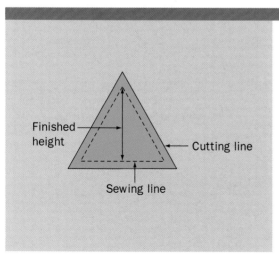

Finished height — Cutting line — Sewing line

1

Equilateral triangles have a 60 degree angle at each corner and measure the same length along each of their three sides. They are used in many quilt blocks, but we often associate them with the traditional Pyramids pattern, a One Patch design made entirely of equilateral triangles. **The height of an equilateral triangle is the distance from the midpoint of one side to the tip of the angle directly above it.** Add ¾ inch to the triangle's finished height to calculate the width to cut parent strips.

Equilateral triangle: Strip width = finished height + ¾"

2

Cut a strip of fabric to the appropriate width. To prepare the strip for cutting equilateral triangles, align the 60 degree line of your rotary ruler with the bottom edge of your strip (you'll work from the right-hand end of the strip). **Cut along the side of the ruler to establish a 60 degree cut edge on the fabric.** Discard the cut-off end, or add it to your scrap bin.

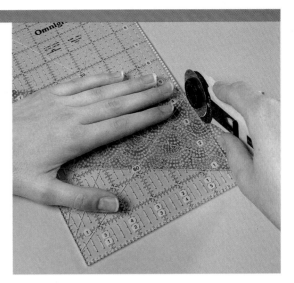

3

Rotate the ruler, aligning its other 60 degree line with the bottom edge of the strip. **Position the right edge of the ruler so that it intersects the top corner created by the first cut. Cut along the side of the ruler to separate the triangle.** To cut more triangles, continue rotating the ruler back and forth between the 60 degree lines, cutting triangles as you go.

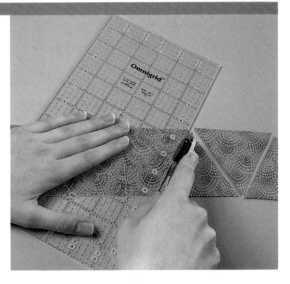

Half-Rectangle

1

Tip

Half-rectangle:
Strip width =
finished height
+ ¹¹/₁₆"
Cut length =
finished length
+ 1⁵/₁₆"

A traditional rectangle (and the half-rectangles cut from it) is twice as long as it is wide. Although the half-rectangle shape isn't quite as common as other shapes in quilting, you will sometimes see it used for star tips or as backgrounds for diamonds. **To calculate the width of parent strips, add ¹¹/₁₆ inch to the finished height of the half-rectangle's short side.** Most rotary rulers aren't marked in ¹/₁₆-inch increments, so estimate the distance by positioning the edge of the fabric midway between two ¹/₈-inch marks.

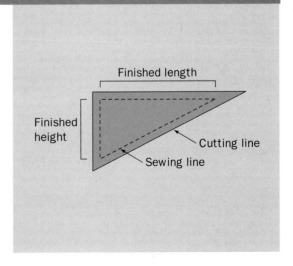

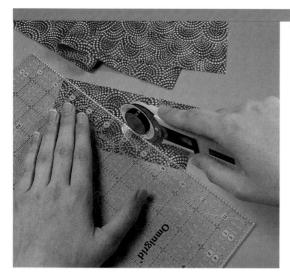

etermine the length of the rectangle you need to cut by adding $1\frac{5}{16}$ inch to the finished length of the half-rectangle. Cut a rectangle from the parent strip. **Then align your rotary ruler to intersect opposite corners of the rectangle, and cut it in half diagonally to create two identical half-rectangles.**

Diamonds

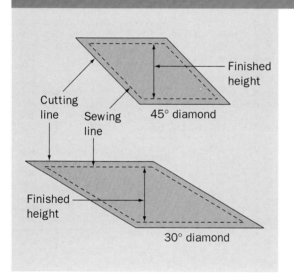

Diamonds are designated by the angles at their narrow points: Quilters usually use 30, 45, and 60 degree diamonds. Think of the shape as a square that has been flattened and tilted (its four sides are still all the same length, but the corner angles have been changed). Diamonds are used in star blocks, basket blocks, and floral designs and by themselves in the Tumbling Blocks quilt. **All diamond types are cut from parent strips that are ½ inch wider than the finished height of the diamond.** Note that the height is measured perpendicular—*not* parallel—to two opposite sides.

Tip

Diamond:
Strip width =
finished
height + ½"

Cut a strip of fabric to the appropriate width. To prepare the strip for cutting diamonds, align the desired angle line (30, 60, or 45 degree) on your ruler with the lower edge of the fabric (work at the right-hand end). **Cut along the side of the ruler to establish the angle.** Discard the cut-off end, or add it to your scrap bin.

Tip

You can glue the cut-off triangles to an index card to catalog the fabrics you used in your quilt.

3

Rotate your mat so that the newly cut angled edge of the strip is to your left. Locate the line on your rotary ruler that matches the cut height of the diamond (the same measurement as your strip width). **Place that line along the angled edge of the fabric, and align the appropriate degree line with the bottom edge of the strip. Cut along the side of the ruler.** If you need more diamonds, continue cutting, but check the angled edge periodically to make sure it is still at the correct angle to the bottom of the strip.

Tip

Always rotate your mat, not your strip or cut patch, so that you won't disturb the fabric or stretch it out of shape.

Hexagon

1

Tip

Hexagon: Strip width = Finished height + ½"

Hexagons, which have six equal sides, are 60 degree diamonds with their narrow points cut off. The Grandmother's Flower Garden is the most well-known quilt pattern that uses hexagons. **To cut hexagons, start with a parent strip that is ½ inch wider than your desired finished height. Cut a 60 degree diamond from the strip,** referring to the instructions for cutting Diamonds on the previous page and above.

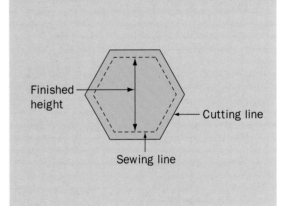

Finished height — Cutting line — Sewing line

2

Tip

The points you remove are equilateral triangles. If they are large enough to be usable, keep them for a future project.

Place the diamond on your cutting mat with its long, narrow tips pointing right and left. **Locate the line on your ruler that equals *half* of the diamond's cutting height (1½ inches in the photograph). Align that measurement on the ruler vertically to pass through the top and bottom points of the diamond.** If you want extra insurance, you can align the 60 degree line with the lower edge of the diamond. Cut along the edge of the ruler to trim off the point. **Rotate your mat 180 degrees and trim the opposite point in the same manner.**

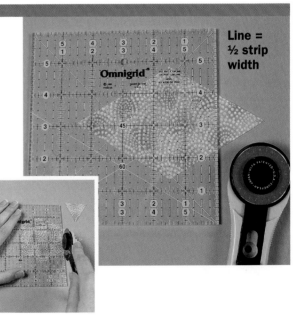

Line = ½ strip width

ROTARY CUTTING UNUSUAL SHAPES

Octagon

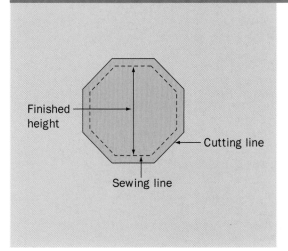

True octagons have eight equal sides. You may see them used as the center of a block, or they can be used to create secondary patterns in the corners where blocks come together. Octagons can be rotary cut quickly and easily by trimming the four corners from a square. **Add ½ inch to the finished height of the octagon, and cut a parent strip to that width.** Cut a square from the parent strip.

Turn the square to the wrong side, and use a sharp marking pencil to lightly draw lines diagonally from corner to corner, forming an X. Place the square wrong side up on the mat, with its corners pointing horizontally and vertically, as if you are setting it on point. **Locate the line on your ruler that equals *half* the square's cutting height, 1¾ inches in the photo. Align this measurement with the vertical drawn line on the square. Trim off the small triangle.** Rotate your mat 180 degrees, and trim off the opposite point in the same manner.

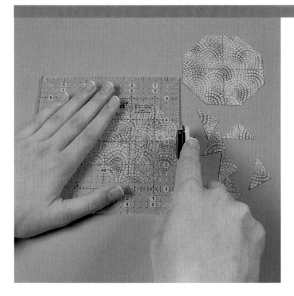

Rotate your mat 90 degrees, align your ruler as you did for the other points, and trim off the third tip. Rotate the mat 180 degrees, and trim off the final point. To check the octagon, measure the distance between opposite straight edges: All four dimensions should be the same.

ROTARY CUTTING UNUSUAL SHAPES

45 Degree Parallelogram

1

Parallelograms resemble stretched diamonds: They have two longer sides and two shorter sides. Parallelograms are often used as roofs of pieced house blocks. **Determine the finished height of the parallelogram by measuring the perpendicular distance between its long sides. Add ½ inch to the finished height, and cut a parent strip that width. Cut the end of the strip at a 45 degree angle, just as you would to prepare the strip for a 45 degree diamond (see page 23).**

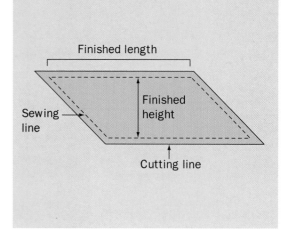

2

Add ¾ inch to the finished length of the parallelogram. Beginning at the cut end of your strip, carefully measure this distance along the top edge of the fabric, and mark the spot with a pencil. Align the 45 degree line with the bottom of the strip and the edge of the ruler with your pencil mark. Cut along the edge of the ruler to cut the parallelogram.

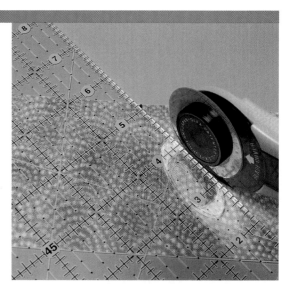

Trapezoid

1

Trapezoids are rectangles with two ends trimmed at opposite angles. Most trapezoids used in quilting have 45 degree ends, such as the background and the spool ends in the traditional Spools block. **Cut a parent strip that is ½ inch wider than the finished height of the trapezoid.**

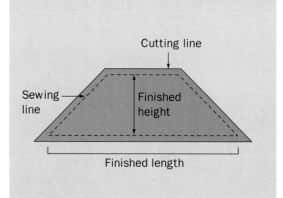

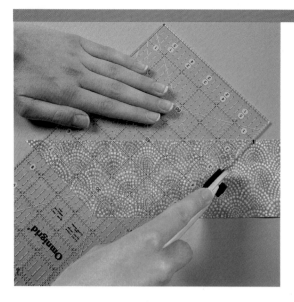

Lay the strip on your cutting mat, and trim one end at a 45 degree angle as you did for the Diamonds on page 23. **Add 1¼ inches to the finished length of the trapezoid's longest edge.** Measure this distance across the top of the strip, and mark the spot with a pencil. **Turn the ruler, and align the opposite 45 degree line with the bottom of the strip and the edge of the ruler with your pencil mark. Cut along the edge of the ruler so that your new angled edge is a mirror image of the first.** To cut more trapezoids, continue marking and cutting, alternating the pencil mark on the top and bottom of the strip.

Kite

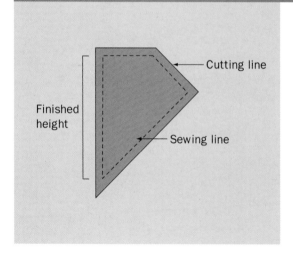

Finished height

← Cutting line

← Sewing line

Kites are half-square triangles with one trimmed corner. They are often used in combination with other shapes to assemble star blocks. Eight kites form an octagon when sewn together along their long edges. **To determine the parent strip width, add ⅞ inch to the finished height of a kite (the measurement of one long side).** Cut a square of that dimension from the parent strip, then cut the square in half diagonally.

Kite:
Strip width = finished height + ⅞"

Place one of the half-square triangles on your cutting mat, its long bias edge facing the top of the mat. Find the line you used to cut parent strips (3 inches in the photo), and place it directly on the left tip of the triangle. **Align one of the horizontal lines on your ruler with the triangle's long edge. Trim the triangle tip that extends beyond the right-hand edge of the ruler.** Discard the tip or add it to your scrap bin.

Scrappy Nine Patch blocks add charm to patchwork quilts, whether they are the main focus or merely filler blocks used with other patterns. Speed up construction without sacrificing the random scrap look by combining strip piecing with individually cut patches. Your quilts will practically jump out, fully pieced, from your scrap basket!

Getting Ready

Nine Patch blocks are a favorite of speed piecers. Traditionally, a Nine Patch is made of three different strip sets, which are then sewn together into a uniform block. But if what you're really going for is the scrappy look, the uniform strip trio isn't going to work for you. To get the best of both worlds—the speed of strip sets, plus the scrappy look—simply combine techniques.

The first thing you must decide is the finished size of your block. A Nine Patch is based on three equal divisions; therefore, a block size that is easily divided by 3 will be the most convenient to calculate. To determine the width of strips to cut, divide the finished block size by 3, then add ½ inch to allow for seam allowances. (For example, for a 6-inch finished block: 6 ÷ 3 = 2 inches; 2 + ½ = 2½ inches.) Use this measurement for cutting your strips and squares as well as for crosscutting the strip sets.

Wide variety of light and dark fabrics, prewashed

Rotary cutter, mat, and acrylic ruler

Sewing machine

Thread to match fabrics

Iron and ironing board

Silk pins

Making Your Nine Patch Blocks

Select some lights and darks from your fabrics, and cut strips from them along the crosswise or lengthwise grain. Make sure you cut carefully: Straight strips will give you straight strip sets and square segments, while wavy strips will give you nothing but trouble!

Tip

For a really scrappy look, sew short strips into longer strips, then join those combination strips into strip sets.

2

Pair your fabric strips so that each pair contains one light and one dark strip. Pin the strips with right sides together, and using ¼-inch seam allowances, sew the pairs into strip sets. **Press the seam allowances toward the dark fabric, being careful not to stretch or distort the strip set during pressing.**

Tip

For more variety, cut strips the full width of the fabric, then cut them in half; mix and match the half-strips when sewing strip sets.

3

Crosscut your strip sets into segments. Remember to use the same width that you cut your strips as the measurement for crosscutting your strip sets. In other words, if your strips were cut 2½ inches wide, cut your segments 2½ inches wide.

4

Cut a variety of dark and light squares, with each side equal to the measurement you used for cutting your strips. If you are cutting a large number of squares, cut strips first, stack them carefully (no more than three at a time), and cut the strips into squares.

Tip

Cut an extra 2½-inch strip each time you have fabric out to cut. In no time, you'll have enough strips for several future scrap blocks.

Select three different cut segments and three cut squares. **Arrange the segments and the squares into a Nine Patch so that lights and darks alternate and a single fabric is not repeated within the block.** If you aren't happy with your first arrangement, substitute other squares or segments until you are pleased with the combination.

If you don't have a design wall for arranging your blocks, tack a piece of batting to a wall or door.

6

With right sides together, align a square with the pieced segment that it will be sewn to. Pin together, keeping raw edges even. **Using a ¼-inch seam allowance, sew the segment and the square together to form a row.** Repeat to assemble the other two rows of the block. If you wish, you may chain piece the combinations one after the other, without cutting the thread until you're done. Press the seam allowances toward the darker squares.

7

Match the seam intersections, pin the rows together carefully, and sew, with a ¼-inch seam allowance, to complete the block. Press the seam allowances in the same direction.

This block is so quick, easy, and fun, you'll be able to make a whole quilt's worth in no time!

SPEEDY, SCRAPPY NINE PATCH

Building Your
Strip-Piecing Skills

In the fast-paced world of speed piecing, the strip set is the workhorse. Simple and straightforward, the strip set goes together quickly, yet it produces intricately pieced squares, rectangles, and diamonds with efficiency and speed. It can breathe new life into triangles and wedges and create settings and borders with instant pizzazz. Take a look at our suggestions for how to use strip sets in your quilts, then explore their versatility on your own!

Getting Ready

The success of any strip-pieced project depends on good basic technique. Review "Accuracy Guaranteed," starting on page 16, to prepare and cut your fabric, then follow these tips for making sure your neatly cut strips are precisely pieced and perfectly pressed.

• Place two strips right sides together, aligning the edges to be sewn. Pin securely.

• Use a ¼-inch patchwork foot (or other stitching guide) to ensure an *exact, consistent* ¼-inch seam allowance.

• To prevent unraveling when crosscutting the seams, adjust the stitch length on your machine to approximately 15 stitches per inch.

• Press your strip set after each strip is added—don't wait until you've sewn more than two strips together to press them.

• Press each seam *as it is sewn,* before opening up the strips to press the seam allowances to one side. This sets the seam and helps ease out any gathers or puckers. Then, open the strips, and press seam allowances toward the darker fabric.

• If joining more than two strips, begin stitching from the opposite end as you add each subsequent strip to the strip set. This helps minimize warping or curving of the strip set. (*Note:* Many quilters prefer the opposite method, sewing from the same end each time. Try it out on your machine and see which method gives you the best results.)

• Press the completed strip set. Make sure the strips are straight and even, using a shot of steam if necessary. Finish with a light application of spray starch to restore a nice, crisp finish. Allow the fabric to dry completely before making the first subcut.

Strip-Set Applications

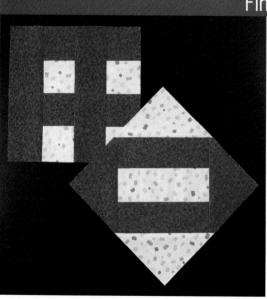

Find the Strip Set in Your Block

Countless traditional quilt blocks are adaptable for strip-piecing techniques. How do you determine if *your* favorite is a likely candidate?

Examine the block carefully. **If the entire block is pieced from squares and rectangles that form an overall pattern or a repeating unit, it is a candidate for strip piecing.**

Perhaps the block is pieced from squares and rectangles *in combination* with other shapes. Study *each section* of the block for repeating shapes. Sometimes you can combine strip piecing those units with other traditional piecing methods.

Four Patch Block

Tip

Use the Four Patch block on its own, or use it as a component in a larger, more complex block.

For many quilters, the most familiar strip-set application is the basic Four Patch unit.

To make it, piece a strip set from two strips of equal width, cut from fabrics of contrasting color and/or value. Subcut the strip set into segments measuring the cut width of each individual strip. (For example, cut a strip set made from 2½-inch-wide strips into 2½-inch segments.)

Arrange two segments so that the colors (or values) are opposite one another. Place them right sides together, pin carefully to match the center seam, sew, and press.

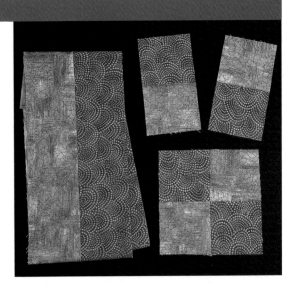

Nine Patch Block

Construct a basic Nine Patch unit by building *two different* strip sets from two contrasting fabrics. Cut each fabric into three strips of equal width. Arrange and sew the strips into two sets of three strips: dark/light/dark and light/dark/light.

Cut two segments from one strip set and one from the other. (Again, cut each segment the same measurement as one cut strip.) **Arrange the strips in three rows, with the odd strip as the middle row.** Pin carefully to match the seams, sew, and press.

Basic Irish Chain Block

Any number of strips can be joined to form a strip set. For example, the Irish Chain—even in its more complex double and triple versions—can be entirely strip pieced, eliminating the need to cut and stitch dozens of individual squares.

The "checkerboard" block of the Irish Chain requires three different strip sets, five strip sets altogether. It is the order in which the strips are pieced and the segments are arranged that determines the finished appearance of the block.

Alternate Irish Chain Block

As in the Irish Chain block, the alternate block is made from strips that vary in width. The finished size of the center strip is three times the finished width of the outer strip sets (don't forget to add seam allowances!). While quilters may have appliquéd hundreds of individual corner squares onto plain alternate blocks at one time, that task is now done with quick, efficient, and accurate rotary-cutting and speed-piecing techniques.

Tip

Experiment with strips of varying widths to create strip sets that you can arrange into your own original designs.

Rail Fence Variations

1

Rail Fence is super-easy to strip piece: It uses a basic strip set cut into square segments. The consistent placement of the colored strips along with the overall arrangement of the blocks give the pattern its simple impact.

The block is traditionally cut from a strip set of either three or four strips. Divide the desired finished size of the block by the number of strips in the strip set. Cut strips to this width *plus ½ inch for seam allowances.* **Piece the strips; then cut segments equal to the width of the strip set. Arrange the blocks with segments alternating in a vertical, then horizontal direction.**

2

A fun variation on the Rail Fence adds movement to the block. By offsetting the cut segments, you get a stair-step effect. Sew together rows of segments, alternating their direction. **Then, sew the rows together, offsetting each row by half a segment.** To finish, trim the edges or remove the extra partial strip sets with a seam ripper.

Tip

Save the trimmed half-segments for another use!

BUILDING YOUR STRIP-PIECING SKILLS

3

For an interesting alternative, cut the strip-pieced Rail Fence segments on point. Multiply the desired finished size of the square by 1.414 to find its diagonal measurement. Add ½ inch for seam allowances, then piece a strip set with this overall width.

Make a template the finished size of the square segment, plus ½ inch for seam allowances. Draw a pencil line to divide the template diagonally in half. **Position the template on point on the strip set so that the diagonal line is parallel to a seam line. Trace and cut a square.** Press with a touch of spray starch, and stay stitch ⅛ inch inside the raw outer edge to stabilize the bias.

4

These diagonally striped Rail Fence segments can be arranged in any number of variations to create exciting new designs. Turn them so that the diagonals face in one direction. Arrange the blocks in mirror-image format to create chevrons or zigzags. Rotate them to create interesting four-block combinations or overall square-within-a-square designs, similar to the familiar Barn Raising Log Cabin set. Because the blocks have been pieced and cut on point, there's no need for diagonal assembly (with setting triangles) to finish the quilt top.

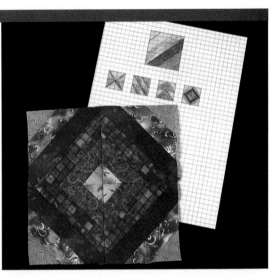

Rectangle Segments

As you become attuned to analyzing blocks for opportunities to strip piece, you'll find that **many blocks incorporate units composed of rectangles.**

To strip piece units for the Paths and Stiles block, determine the size of the finished rectangle unit. Figure the finished width of the individual rectangle, then add ½ inch for seam allowances. Cut strips of this width from the appropriate fabrics, strip piece, and press. Subcut the strip set into segments equal to the measurement of the finished unit plus ½ inch for seam allowances.

Rectangles and Squares

Many familiar designs include both repeating square *and* repeating rectangle units in a single block. Occasionally these strip-pieced rectangle and square units comprise the entire design; sometimes they combine with other single shapes or pieced units.

Analyze these blocks to identify the areas that can be strip pieced. Determine the finished size of each individual unit or grid and the number and variety of strip sets needed. Base the cut width of the required strips on the unit size. Don't forget to add seam allowances!

Strip-Pieced Diamonds

Increase the versatility of the strip set by slicing it at a *45 degree angle* to assemble the pieced points for Lone Star and other eight-pointed star blocks.

Figure the width of an *individual* diamond; add ½ inch seam allowance. Cut strips of each fabric to this width, then piece strips *in order*

See pages 23–24 for instructions on figuring out diamond size.

for *each* diagonal row of the larger diamond. Align the 45 degree line on your ruler with a seam line on the strip set. Cut segments equal to the cut width of the diamond. Arrange and sew the strips to form the large diamond.

Pieced Triangles

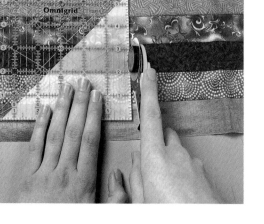

Strip sets can be cut into shapes other than squares or rectangles. Try your hand at cutting strip-pieced half-square triangles. Cut your triangles using a ruler with a 45 degree angle line. When cutting the long edge, align the 45 degree line with one of the seam lines—not the raw edge—for the most accurate cut. **Or make a template to cut around.** If you're concerned about exact placement, mark the strip positions on the template.

BUILDING YOUR STRIP-PIECING SKILLS

37

Pieced Wedges

1

Tip

The strip-pieced version of a Kaleidoscope block is called Spider Web. Piece strip sets as wide as the height of the wedge from peak to base.

Jazz up a Kaleidoscope block with strip sets. To draft a block on paper, draw two long perpendicular lines. Draw two more lines, bisecting the first two at exactly 45 degree angles. From the center, measure out the same distance on each line and mark that point. Connect the points from line to line to create the octagon. Extend the lines to add corners completing the finished size block. Cut out one triangle wedge to make a template, adding ¼ inch seam allowances all around. Align the base of the template with the long edge of the strip set, cut eight wedges, and assemble the block.

2

Tip

Rotary rulers now come in all shapes and sizes, including triangles and wedges. Use these in place of templates!

To give your Spider Web block a twist, spin your template. **After cutting each triangle, flip the template, aligning it with the strip set's opposite raw edge.** Mark and cut the next piece, continuing to alternate from edge to edge. If you work carefully, you can position (or "butt") the template to create common cutting lines. Not only will you save fabric, but you'll have two different arrangements of strips.

Use Color to Your Advantage

Create different effects with strip sets by way of fabric selection. Cool colors and grayed tones have a serene, calming effect, while bright, warmer hues stir visual excitement. Mix high-contrast lights and darks, warm and cool colors, brights and tones to create movement and "sizzle."

Suggest motion or depth by grading fabrics from light to dark. Use a single color or a mixed palette, in prints or solids, as long as the strip-to-strip contrast is subtle (see "Strip-Pieced Color Gradations" on page 42).

Strip in Corner Squares

Don't limit strip piecing to blocks alone. Strip sets can be adapted to create super setting components, adding maximum impact for a minimum investment of time and effort. **Substitute strip-pieced Four Patch and Nine Patch blocks for the plain corner squares customarily placed at the intersection of sashing strips.** Use your imagination! Sometimes these simply pieced corner squares create wonderful secondary designs as they touch the corners of adjacent blocks.

Strippy Sashing

Sashing may also be cut from strip sets of two, three, or more strips. Determine the desired finished width of the sashing strip and add ½ inch for the seam allowances. This is the size your pieced strip set should measure when it is assembled. Individual strips may be cut all the same width or in varying widths, depending upon the requirements of your design. Cut the strip set into sashing segments of the appropriate length. Don't forget to include seam allowances.

Piece sashing strip sets from the same two or three fabrics for a more formal look. For a scrappy look, mix and match as many as you please!

Strippy Sashing Turned Sideways

Here's another great strip-pieced sashing option. **Cut your segments so that the strips run perpendicular to the block edges.** With stripes this way, you can get a fresh, funky, or folk-art look.

Measure the unfinished blocks you wish to sash. Using *at least* six different strips, piece a strip set. Combine individual strips the same width or of varying widths, depending upon the look you wish to achieve. Make the strip set as wide as necessary to equal the block measurement. Determine how wide you want the sashing strip to be, add ½ inch for seam allowances, and cut segments from the strip set to equal this measurement.

Tip

Consider using cross-pieced sashing to surround simple, large blocks or appliqué blocks with lots of empty space.

Tip

BUILDING YOUR STRIP-PIECING SKILLS

39

Pieced Corner Squares plus Sashing

Need to jazz up a rather sedate collection of blocks? **Pair Nine Patch corner squares with three-strip sashes!**

See "Nine Patch Block" on page 34 center to assemble the basic Nine Patch, then piece additional strip sets identical to the middle row of the Nine Patch. Cut the new strips to use as sashing, and assemble the quilt top as usual. Where the corner squares meet the strip-pieced sashes, a wonderful positive/negative effect results. This setting is also ideal for showcasing theme panels, vintage embroidery, or large squares of those extra-special fabrics you can't bear to cut.

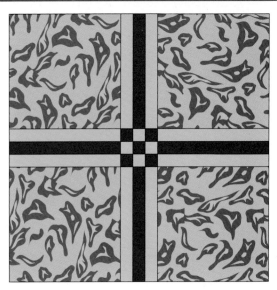

Strippy Borders

Strip-pieced borders make wonderful frames for quilts and wallhangings. Piece strip sets, then subcut segments equal to the finished width of the border *plus seam allowances*. Join the segments to form borders of the required length.

Depending upon your preference, you can cut the individual strips the same width or in varying widths. Just remember that you'll want each panel to begin and end with a complete strip. Do a little figuring to determine how many strips you'll need and how wide to cut them.

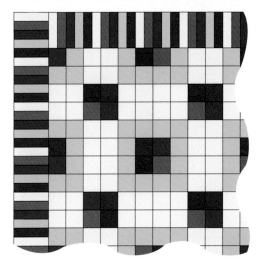

Borders with a Twist

Let yourself think outside the box when you're designing your borders. Just because strip sets are straight and square doesn't mean they have to be used that way! Try Four Patch or Nine Patch checkerboards on their own or mixed with strip-pieced rectangles. Combine strips of varying widths, either in repeat or random patterns, then turn them horizontally, vertically, diagonally . . . or combine them all!

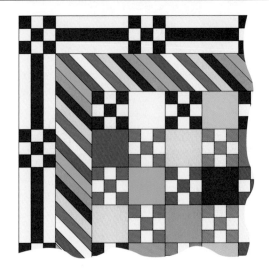

The Quilter's
Problem Solver

Cutting Concerns

Problem	Solution
Your rotary mat—which is supposed to be the "self-healing" type—is developing nicks and grooves.	One of the worst enemies your cutting mat can have is a dull rotary blade. A dull blade doesn't cut cleanly, and it embeds bits of fiber and fabric lint into the board as you cut. This prevents the mat from healing and allows those nicks and grooves to worsen. Always work with a sharp rotary blade! You'll cut more accurately and prolong the life of your cutting mat.
Threads and lint are building up in the crevices of your rotary mat.	Keep your mat and cutter in tiptop condition to prolong the life of your mat. ❏ Always use a rotary cutter with a sharp blade that will cut through the threads, not force them into the mat. ❏ A gadget called a Mat Smoother removes threads and fibers and smoothes the nicks and grooves in your cutting mat. ❏ Try this tip we picked up on the Internet: Use a crepe rubber cement pickup (available at art supply stores) to clean your rotary mat. Rub it across the surface like an eraser to remove embedded lint and threads.

Skill Builder

Add a whole new design dimension to your quilt with strip-pieced bindings. Cut a variety of strips in either the same or various widths. Arrange the strips in any order that you please. Make a strip set, then cut segments to the desired width of your binding—either straight or on the diagonal. Join your segments into one continuous length to create the required binding length. Press the seams open to distribute the bulk more evenly. *Note:* Sew slowly when you attach the binding, since it will have more seams than usual.

Try This!

Crosscutting lots of strip sets dulls the blade of your rotary cutter quickly.

Restore dull rotary blades with the help of a rotary blade sharpener, available through your local quilt shop or favorite mail-order source. It includes a built-in emery and comes in three sizes to accommodate regular, heavy-duty, and extra-large blades. Simply drop the blade into the holder, screw on the handle, and twist. Or, for a minimal fee and return postage, you can send blades out to be resharpened. See "Resources" on page 125 for additional information.

I t's hard to resist the hand-dyed fabrics available at quilt shows, in shops, and by mail order. Collect a wonderful stash of colorful, textured-looking fabrics in shades of one color or a luscious spectrum. Watching colors flow into each other in a carefully planned gradation turns even a simple, traditional quilt pattern that you have used many times into a fresh, new, and exciting one.

Getting Ready

The important thing in creating a value gradation is that your colors move smoothly into one another. Hand-dyed fabrics are perfect for this. Many companies who make these sell them in bundles of six to eight gradated colors for this purpose. See "Resources" on page 125 for mail-order sources.

To use hand-dyed fabric efficiently, choose a block or design that consists of medium-size patches. Large pieces waste fabric, and very small pieces lose a lot of fabric in seam allowances.

Choose other fabrics that coordinate with the hand-dyed ones to extend and complement them. A print or batik fabric need contain only two shades of the color in the dyed value gradation to work. If you are mixing light with dark hand-dyed fabrics, rinse the darker colors to make sure all excess dye is removed.

Uncomfortable about cutting into these pricier hand-dyed fabrics? "Practice" your gradations first with less expensive fabrics—tiny prints or tone-on-tone solid substitutes.

Moving with Gradations

1

The first step is to alter your existing quilt pattern using strip piecing. On graph paper, draw the block pattern, lattice, border, or background area that will be filled with strip piecing. Determine what direction the strips will run. Draw parallel lines that complement the scale of the piecing units, appliqué motifs, or borders that you are using.

Tip

Graph paper comes in many sizes. Most quilters find that four squares to the inch (or ¼ inch) works well.

STRIP-PIECED COLOR GRADATIONS

2

Make copies of the design using tracing paper or a copy machine. **Use colored pencils to fill in the value gradations.** Try different arrangements such as light to dark returning to light, or light to dark starting over at light. Use good-quality colored pencils with soft lead, and you should be able to color eight values using the same pencil.

3

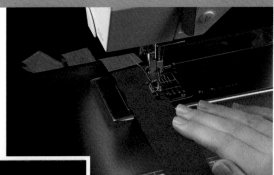

Referring to your drawing, cut strips of fabric to the width desired (don't forget to add ½ inch for seam allowances), and sew them into strip sets. **Chain piecing makes the process go faster;** refer to your drawing to make sure your strips stay in order.

Press your strip set after adding each strip. First, press the seam as sewn, then open out the top strip and press the entire length of the strips, gently easing out any small pleats or creases. This ensures that your seams are smooth and flat and helps keep your strips straight.

4

If you are using your strip sets within a patch, cut the individual units you need. Be sure to cut the strip sets carefully, following your original design. **It may be useful the first few times you cut to make a template and mark the placement of the strips on it.** After you have worked with the strip sets for a while, you can switch to a rotary ruler.

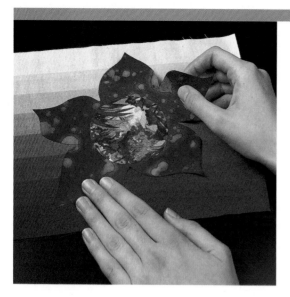

Strip-pieced gradated backgrounds add excitement and movement to simple appliqué blocks. Decide on your color scheme, then make strip sets and crosscut them into segments. Reassemble the segments, playing with the arrangement until you find one that suits your appliqué shape. Try placing them side by side, sliding the segments up and down to create a Bargello effect, and rotating every other segment to create opposing value order. Press the newly constructed background piece, trim the edges, and appliqué the motifs to the fabric.

Tip

Handle your cut segments carefully so you don't pull out the stitching.

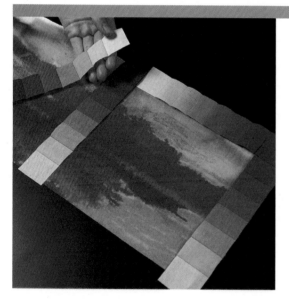

Gradated lattice can really add pizzazz to a quilt. Try featuring a snazzy batik or hand-painted fabric as a plain block, then highlighting it with strip-pieced gradated lattice. Make your strip sets, cut them into segments the width of your lattice (plus ½ inch for seam allowances), then lay them out with the blocks and decide how you want the values to run and meet at the intersections.

Tip

A Polaroid camera is a helpful tool. You'll keep track of different arrangements as you play with design options.

A gradated lengthwise border is a stunning frame for your quilt. Depending on the size of the quilt, you may need to purchase yardage of your hand-dyed fabrics. Figure the length you'll need for your borders, and make sure you take seam allowances into consideration. Try both light to dark and dark to light. You may even want to bind your quilt in bias-cut, strip-pieced gradations!

STRIP-PIECED COLOR GRADATIONS

Once Upon a
Triangle Square

Triangle squares are well loved as basic building blocks of piecing. Many familiar patterns consist partially or entirely of a square, sewn from two triangles of contrasting fabrics. Triangles create a sense of motion and complexity, yet they are simple to piece using either traditional or quick methods. Are you a beginner quiltmaker? Triangle squares are a great starting point. Are you interested in playing with color value, interesting fabrics, or innovative settings? Triangle squares offer limitless possibilities for experimentation.

Getting Ready

There are several methods for constructing triangle squares. The simplest method is to cut squares, cut them in half diagonally to form triangles, and sew two different triangles together along the long bias edge. If you don't want to bother with bias edges, there are papers commercially available that are printed with lines for sewing two fabrics together to make up triangle squares. (See "Resources" on page 125 for product information.) These grids can also be drawn directly on fabric.

To create simple patchwork designs using these triangle-square units, start with two contrasting fabrics. Make up at least a dozen triangle squares, then set up a design wall so you can play with the arrangements and explore the endless possibilities these simple pieced units can produce.

What You'll Need

Fabrics in light and dark values

Rotary cutter, mat, and acrylic ruler

Silk pins

Sewing machine

¼" presser foot

Iron and ironing board

Design wall

Simple Triangle Squares

1

Sort your fabrics into light and dark piles. Generally, each triangle square will be made from one light and one dark fabric. This allows maximum contrast and helps you see your emerging design as you arrange the squares into blocks and quilts. Medium-value fabrics shouldn't be avoided, though—just make sure when you pair up a medium with either a light or a dark fabric that the fabrics contrast well with each other.

Tip

Looking through a red-colored viewer, or value finder, will help you obtain good contrasts—especially with medium-value fabrics.

Tip

Layer your light and dark fabrics with right sides together, then cut squares and triangles. Your pairs of triangles will be perfectly aligned for sewing.

To cut triangles using your ruler and rotary cutter, first determine the finished size (of each side) of the square you want to have in the end. Add ⅞ inch to that measurement, and cut squares to that size. **Lay your ruler diagonally across the squares and cut them in half, giving you two triangles from each square.**

Tip

Stick to silk pins for chain piecing: You can sew right over them.

Pin your triangle pairs together along the long bias edge (the edge you just cut), placing one silk pin at the beginning, another at the end. You may wish to insert a pin or two in between as well. **As you sew the triangles together, hold onto the head of the pin to guide the triangle points under the presser foot smoothly.** This helps keep your seam line straight the entire length of the bias edge. Chain piecing the pairs (sewing one right after the other) saves you time and thread.

Pressing is critical when you're making triangle squares. First, place the sewn unit on your ironing board with the darker triangle on top. Press the seam as it was sewn, without opening up the triangles. This helps keep the sewn seam straight and "sets" the bias edge in place so it's less likely to pull out of shape. **Then, unfold the top triangle completely, and press your new square gently so you don't stretch it out of shape.**

Use a small pair of scissors to trim the "dog ears" even with the edge of your square. This will help when you sew the units together.

Designing Blocks with Triangle Squares

1

Sometimes it's fun—and creative!—to start merely with favorite fabrics or colors rather than picking out a block or quilt design ahead of time. **Make up triangle squares in whatever quantity and size you're interested in working with, then just play with them on a design wall or a flat surface.** Try turning them various ways, combining them with other shapes of similar size, and combining different sizes of triangle squares. Read on for more ideas!

2

Sometimes the simplest blocks can be the most effective. This Broken Dishes block is nothing more than a Four Patch, each square replaced with a triangle square. The combinations for this block are fun to play with, too. **Four blocks placed together in one combination makes a twirling pinwheel design; placed another way, a star pops out of your new block!**

Tip

Use graph paper or a computer design program to substitute triangle squares for plain squares in your favorite quilt blocks.

3

Just as you can substitute triangle squares in a Four Patch, you can do the same in a Nine Patch. **This Wild Geese block is made completely of triangle squares, arranged with the dark triangular birds "flying as a flock" in the same direction.** This pattern is also fun to do in scrappy prints and is often seen turned on point, in sparkling colors, or as a charm quilt.

Tip

Try setting blocks with contrasting corner triangles side by side for an interesting secondary design.

4

Here's another Nine Patch variation, with a slight twist. **This Friendship Star is made of eight triangle squares surrounding one plain center square.** The difference here is the placement of the lights and darks of the triangle squares. This combination makes a pinwheel star on an octagonal background.

5

As you add more triangle squares to your design, you also add more movement and play. This Jack-in-the-Box block has a center pinwheel, spinning inside a larger X. **At first glance, the shapes look difficult to piece, but when you break the block down into a 4 × 4 block, you see that it's simply made of 16 identical triangle squares.**

6

Adding more patches also allows you to add different colors, textures, and prints to your block without overwhelming the design. **This Comet block uses triangle squares in light and dark combinations but places low-contrast triangle squares on the outer edges of the block.** The result is fun—a background that dances along with the central whirling design without distracting from it.

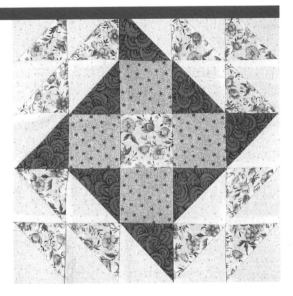

There are other blocks that can be made of triangle squares as well. The traditional Flying Geese unit is made of two half-square triangles sewn to a quarter-square triangle. (Quarter-square triangles have the bias along the two short sides. A square is cut in half diagonally both ways to obtain four of these triangles.) **If you want scrappy geese, make your Flying Geese from triangle squares instead.** Or, use identical triangle squares for "mock" Flying Geese.

Tip

To cut quarter-square triangles, start with a square 1¼ inches larger than the finished size of the triangle's long edge. Cut in half diagonally twice.

Tip

When working with bias edges, pin well, and sew slowly to make sure that your seam line stays straight.

Just as you can replace plain squares in blocks with triangle squares, you can also replace part of a triangle square with a pieced triangle. **This Pinwheel block gets a boost when one half-square triangle in each pair is replaced with one pieced from two quarter-square triangles sewn to-gether.** The Double Pinwheel almost seems to spin faster!

Combining different sizes of triangle squares within the same block really expands your design options. Only a little math is required: Just double the finished size of your small triangle square for a larger one, and you have an easy set of building blocks for new combinations of designs. (Remember, no matter what the finished size of your triangle square is, always add ⅞ inch to find your cut size.) **This 9-inch Double T block uses 1½-inch and 3-inch triangle squares.**

This Flying Birds block is essentially made of only one triangle square! One-half of the block is a solid triangle; the other half is a triangle made up of three smaller triangle squares, plus three single half-triangles.

Tip

Use fabrics that echo the size of the triangle—small-scale prints for tiny triangles; large-scale prints in larger ones.

Here's a different arrangement of multiple sizes of triangle squares. **Instead of doubling the size of the small unit, triple it, then surround the large triangle square with small ones, as in this Lady of the Lake block.** For a less formal look, feature large prints in the center of the block and coordinating scrappy prints in the block's "border."

Basket blocks come in so many variations, and they're great fun to make. One of the most popular "on-point" blocks (blocks used in a diagonal setting), **basket patterns usually feature triangle squares in combination with rectangles or other shape patches.**

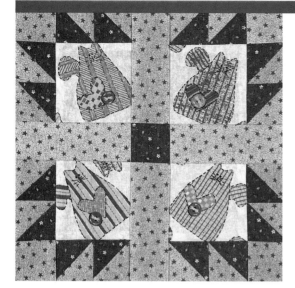

If you're up for a little more of a challenge, try a slightly more complicated block, such as a Bear's Paw. **This block uses the triangle squares as a jaunty framing device around four large squares.** The Bear's Paw block works well in a traditional two-color quilt. Here, the four fat cat motifs suggest that this block be renamed cat's claws!

Tip

Pointy triangle squares are the perfect frame for a conversation print motif.

The Indian Trails block, like Lady of the Lake, uses smaller triangle squares to frame a large triangle square. Set together, these blocks spin, move, and point in all directions. Monochromatic colors calm the block, but wild, bright colors would produce a riotous block demanding the viewer's attention.

Triangle Squares as Setting Elements

Triangle squares alternating with Four Patch blocks can turn the mundane into a masterpiece. Arranging triangle squares with Four Patch blocks as shown results in a Jacob's Ladder block. This works up quickly into a stunning quilt with unlimited design possibilities.

Similar to Jacob's Ladder, the triangle square can be used as an alternate block for a dramatic diagonal setting. Facing the triangle squares all in the same direction gives a Sunshine and Shadows look to a quilt, with the diagonal lines adding a sense of movement. Not only that, but you get a "diagonal" look to your set without having to use setting triangles!

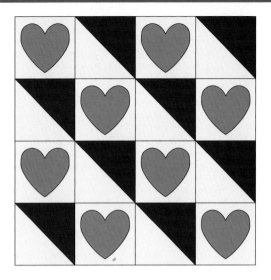

Once you stop to analyze the construction of this Zigzag pattern, you'll see that it's made entirely of triangle squares! This quilt gives you yet another way to get diagonal movement without setting your blocks on point. And with a little careful planning of your colors and placement, you can get a gradation of color that moves across the quilt.

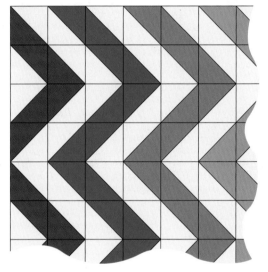

A sawtooth border adds pizzazz and motion to the outer edges of a quilt. Measure the sides of your quilt top and divide that by the size of triangle square you want to make, rounding up to determine the number of triangle squares you will need. Add a narrow inner border if necessary to make the quilt fit the border. Choose fabrics that coordinate with the center of your quilt top and place them around your quilt. As you arrange the border, play with the direction of the triangle squares.

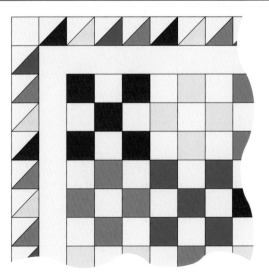

The Quilter's
Problem Solver

Getting Accurate Triangle Squares

Problem	Solution
Sewn triangle squares aren't square at all.	Make sure you are cutting your squares exactly in half. If your ruler slips just a bit, you're going to be sewing together pieces that aren't the right shape, and you'll end up with out-of-square triangle squares. Try adding sandpaper dots or another nonslip device to the underside of your ruler (see page 19).
	Check your seam allowance. Sew with a scant ¼-inch seam, and make sure your sewing is even all the way along the bias edge.
	Press carefully. After pressing the seam, open up the top triangle completely, hold it in place with your fingers, and set the iron carefully on the seam.

ONCE UPON A TRIANGLE SQUARE

Skill Builder

If you have a box or bundle of fat eighths (9 inches × 22 inches) of fabric, turn the whole assortment into 2½-inch triangle squares. On the design wall, lay out as many different blocks as possible, using two or three different fabric combinations in each block and striving for maximum contrast and visual impact. By limiting yourself to the fabrics contained in the packaged assortment and to a small scale, you will gain practice in working with color and value as well as in sewing precisely.

Try This!

Whenever you make a block or quilt from triangle squares, sew a few extra and store them in a box protected from sunlight. When your box is full, try making a quilt from all of the various squares. A sampler of different-size blocks might be fun, or you can cut the larger squares down to smaller sizes. Use a design wall to experiment with different ideas. Add multicolored or black lattice to help tie all the fabric colors together.

Double-Stitched
Triangle Squares

A sk two quilters the best way to quick piece half-square triangle units, and you're bound to get three answers! There are so many ways to make triangle squares, and all (or almost all!) achieve the same end product. This one, the double-stitched triangle squares method, gives you accurate triangle squares, with no grids to mark and no paper foundations to remove.

Getting Ready

Double-stitched triangle squares result in traditional half-square triangles without having to cut and sew triangles together. To make them, you cut strips of fabric on the bias and place them right sides together. Stitch both long edges, using ¼-inch seam allowances, to form a flat tube. After sewing, rotary cut the tube into triangles. Unfold, press, and you'll have perfect triangle squares!

Refer to the chart at right for some common finished sizes of half-square triangles. You can also cut wider strips, make oversized triangle squares, and trim them after pressing for perfectly square and accurate results.

To calculate other sizes, here's the formula to use with your calculator. Take the desired finished size of the triangle square and multiply it by itself (square it). Divide that number by 2 and take the square root of that answer. Add 0.625 (⅝ inch) to that; round to the nearest ⅛ inch to get the width to cut the bias strips.

For a finished size triangle square of:	Cut a bias strip this width:
2"	2"
2½"	2⅜"
3"	2¾"
3½"	3⅛"
4"	3½"

Strips to Squares

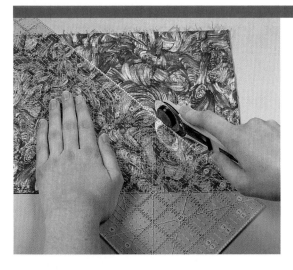

1

Straighten one long edge of your fabric, as described on page 18.

Lay your piece of fabric, unfolded, across your cutting mat, placing your newly straightened edge at the bottom (closest to you). **Align a ruler's 45 degree angle line with the bottom edge of the fabric.** Cut away the corner along the bias of the fabric.

2

If your fabric is a directional plaid or stripe and you want the lines to appear straight in the finished triangle square, the edge of the fabric may not be your best guide. Many of these fabrics are printed or woven off-grain or off-kilter with the fabric's edge. **Instead, align the 45 degree angle line on your ruler with the pattern (for printed fabrics) or with the grain (for woven fabrics).**

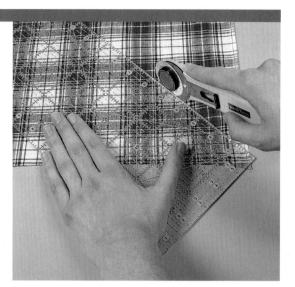

Tip

If you stack two fabrics right sides together, they will be ready to be joined as soon as they are cut into strips.

3

Rotate your cutting mat so that the cut edge is on your left (for right-handers). **Find the line on your ruler that corresponds to the desired width of your bias strip. Align this line with the angled edge you just cut.** Cut strips to that width along the entire length of your fabric.

Tip

Complete all the steps for one set of strips first, so you'll know exactly how many triangle squares each produces.

4

If you haven't done so, stack your pairs of bias strips right sides together. Take care handling these pieces with stretchy edges. **Stitch along one long edge, using a ¼-inch seam allowance.** Chain piece the bias strips by feeding them into the machine one behind the other to save time and thread.

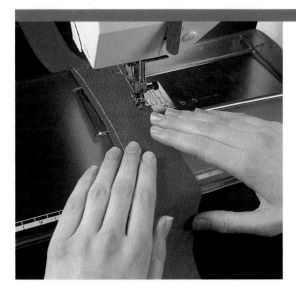

Feed your chain of strip pairs into the sewing machine in the opposite direction. **Stitch along the other long edge, again using a ¼-inch seam allowance.** *Note:* Depending on your machine, you may get better results if you sew in the same direction, beginning at the same end as you did before. You may want to try it both ways on scrap fabric strips to see which gives you the most evenly stitched seams along both edges.

Tip

Use a thread color that contrasts slightly with your fabric to make it easier to evaluate the quality of your stitching line.

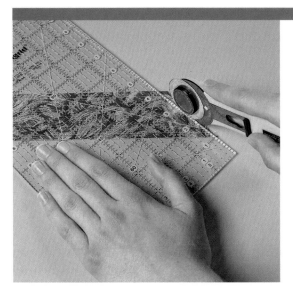

Cut the chain of double-stitched bias strips apart from each other. Lay one strip on your cutting mat. **Place the 45 degree line on your ruler along the long edge of the strip, and cut the right end at a perfect 45 degree angle.**

Tip

Bias stretches easily. Handle these strips gently—and as little as possible—so they don't become misshapen.

Turn your mat 90 degrees or one-quarter turn, so the angle you just cut is facing toward you. **Place your ruler on the strip so that the 45 degree angle line aligns with the long edge of the strip and the edge of the ruler passes exactly through the wide angle on the strip.** Cut along the edge of the ruler to create your first triangle pair.

Tip

Always rotate your mat, not your fabric, so that your strip won't become distorted or stretched out of shape.

DOUBLE-STITCHED TRIANGLE SQUARES

Tip

The Brooklyn Revolver, a turntable cutting mat, is perfect for rotating and cutting triangle pairs.

8

Rotate the mat 90 degrees and place the ruler as you did in Step 6, with the 45 degree angle line along the lower long edge of the strip. Make sure that the ruler is placed so that you can cut along the right-hand edge (for a right-handed cutter). Cut another triangle pair. Continue to rotate the mat, cutting triangle pairs, until you have cut as many pairs as possible from your strip.

9

Carefully pick up a triangle pair, being careful not to stretch it out of shape. **Use a small pair of scissors to nip off the protruding triangles (dog ears).** This way, when you press, the seams are less likely to stretch out of shape.

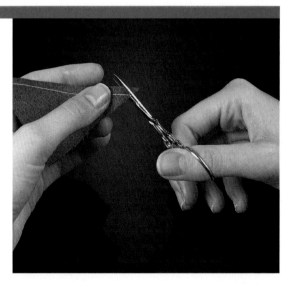

10

Open the triangles carefully, pulling out the few stitches that cross the triangle tip opposite your seam allowance. **Working carefully so as not to stretch the bias edges out of shape, press the seam allowances toward the darker fabric.**

The Quilter's
Problem Solver

De-Stressing Triangle Squares

Problem	Solution
When you press the triangle squares open, you have a small notch in one corner.	Sew another row of stitching, slightly to the inside of the previous line of stitches. This will cover up the notch, but it will also give you a slightly smaller triangle square.
You're short just a few triangle squares to finish your quilt.	When you made the first cut from each piece of fabric, before cutting the bias strips, you cut away a large triangle. Use these to cut shorter bias strips to make the additional triangle squares.

Skill Builder

Here's a way to make scrappy triangle squares when you have scrap triangles to use up.

Cut a bias strip at least ⅜ inch wider than your largest scrap triangle. Use light strips for dark scraps and dark strips for light scraps. Lay your triangles along the edges, as shown in the illustration. Sew seams, leaving ¼-inch seam allowances along both long edges, then cut the pairs apart.

Try This!

Try one of these ideas to get a scrappier look in your triangle squares:

❏ Cut strips from several different light and dark fabrics. Mix and match strips when sewing them together.

❏ Cut your strips in half and pair them in different combinations for more variation.

❏ Separate several lights and several darks into piles. Unfold these fabrics and place the darks right side up and the lights right side down. Cut these fabrics into strips, then pair the light and dark strips randomly.

Fun with
Half-Rectangles

U n-"leash" your creativity! Explore the many possibilities of the half-rectangle with its sharply angled points. In place of the usual triangle square, this elongated pair produces unusual stars, flowers, or even lovable creatures. Designs can range from whimsical and playful to elegant and formal, but all of them are doggone interesting.

Getting Ready

Refer to "Half-Rectangle" on page 22 for instructions and helpful tips on figuring out the size of the rectangle you'll need to cut for your design. Then, following these instructions, carefully cut your rectangle(s) in half diagonally, as indicated. Be especially careful at the corners: If your ruler slips just a little, your half-rectangle will be misshapen, and it will be doubly hard for you to match up the bias (diagonal) edge with the other patches you want to sew it to.

If you're using a loosely woven fabric or one that doesn't have much body, give it a light application of spray starch and press it gently before cutting. This will give it a little more body and make it easier to cut accurately.

What You'll Need

Fabrics, prewashed and pressed

Rotary cutter, mat, and acrylic rulers

Graph paper and colored pencils

Template plastic (optional)

Fine-tip permanent marker or pencil (optional)

Small hole punch or large darning needle (optional)

Silk pins

Sewing machine

Tri-Recs tools (optional)

Design wall

Designing with Half-Rectangles

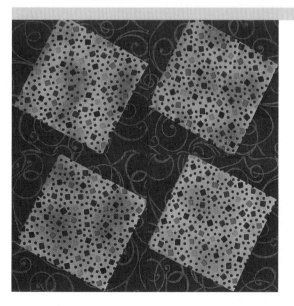

Half-rectangles are fun around a square block to "tip" it a little for a jaunty-looking setting. **Choose any square block or a square of a favorite large-print fabric and sew half-rectangles around it.** The result is a quick, easy quilt that spins and turns.

To calculate the size rectangle you'll need to surround a block, use a calculator to divide the finished block size by 2.236 to get your base number. For the short side of the rectangle, add ½ inch to the base number. For the long side, multiply the base number by 2; then add 1⅛ inches. Round both numbers to the nearest ⅛ inch.

Tip

For maximum spin, use different fabrics for the half-rectangles in the center.

2

Sew half-rectangles together into pairs to take the place of rectangles or two half-square triangles in a design. **As a first step, look for block designs that contain rectangles or half-square triangles, and draw them with half-rectangles instead.** You'll create interesting shapes, and you can even draw your own designs. Each pooch on page 62, for example, would still have four legs if the quiltmaker had simply joined narrow rectangles together, but the pointy feet—not to mention the perky ears and tail—make him so much snappier!

Matching and Sewing Half-Rectangles

1

Tip

Use an extra-fine-tip permanent marker or a thin lead pencil to mark your intersections.

To make sure your half-rectangles match up correctly, mark the ¼-inch seam intersections with dots. If you'll be making several same-size half-rectangles, make a marking template. Cut a half-rectangle out of template plastic just as you did the fabric ones. **Then carefully draw light pencil lines along the bias (diagonal) edge and the two adjacent edges to indicate the sewing lines. Use a small hole punch or a large darning needle to pierce holes through the intersections of the lines.** These will be your marking holes.

2

Tip

Mark dots on dark fabrics using a well-sharpened chalk pencil.

Place the template on the wrong side of each half-rectangle, and mark the dots through the holes you punched or pierced. Place the bias edges together with right sides facing, and line up the marked points. **Place pins through the marked dots, matching both sets of dots carefully.** The tips of the triangles will overhang their mates' corresponding edges.

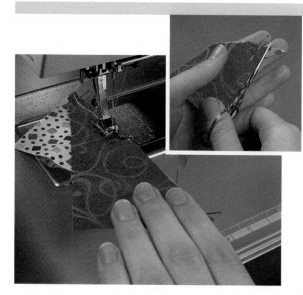

Sewing those bias edges together can be tricky—the narrow points on either end are hard to control. **Nip off the points that hang beyond the other half-rectangle** on either end, pin, and **sew slowly and carefully along the bias edge.**

Press gently to avoid distorting the long bias seam.

Using Tri-Recs Tools

The Tri-Recs tools (see "Resources" on page 125) are two rulers that help you cut and sew a half-rectangle (Recs tool) and a coordinating isosceles triangle (Tri tool) without marking. Both tools have blunt points that eliminate the need to trim "dog ears" when matching pieces.

For half-rectangles, cut strips the same measurement as the unfinished long side of your rectangle. **Align the blunt point of the Recs tool with a long edge of the strip. Cut out a half-rectangle.** Flip the tool upside down for every other half-rectangle.

Tip

Cut out isosceles triangles with the Tri tool using the same method, aligning the blunt point and flipping the tool.

To pin the half-rectangles together, **simply align the bias edges, right sides together, and line up the blunted tips with the edges of the half-rectangles.** Pin securely and sew the bias edge.

Designs for Half-Rectangle Pairs

Star

You can make shimmering star points with half-rectangle pairs. **Construct and align half-rectangle pairs in sets of two pairs. With a busy background fabric, the seam is hardly noticeable.**

If you are using the Tri-Recs tools, you can use the Recs tool for the star points and the Tri tool for the triangular background pieces.

Latticework

Tip

Press seam allowances for half of the half-rectangle pairs in one direction, half in the other direction, to avoid mismatched or bulky seams.

Here's a fun half-rectangle design that will also showcase that favorite print fabric you've been saving for just the right quilt. **In this latticework design, your fabric peeks out from behind the zigzag latticework.** Looks complicated, but if you study the construction, you'll see it's made entirely of half-rectangle pairs.

Mountains

Tip

Make sketches and play with your half-rectangles on a design wall before you begin sewing pairs together.

Here's a quick and easy way to make a stunning landscape quilt, again using a combination of half-rectangle pairs. **By changing the colors of your rectangle pairs as you progress, you can create impressive mountains, sky, and clouds using ordinary fabrics.**

Mistakes and Misshapes

Problem	Solution
Half-rectangles aren't cut evenly.	Ruler slippage is the most common problem. Try using nonslip dots on the underside of your ruler (see page 19). Your rectangle may have been out of square. Check to make sure the strips that you use to cut the rectangles are even throughout their length. Every 6 inches or so, recut a straight edge on your yardage, then continue cutting strips.
Half-rectangle pairs are out of square.	Make sure when sewing that you begin and end very carefully. Because you're sewing two bias edges together, the ends have a tendency to twist away from the feed dogs. Pin the points especially well, and sew slowly. Pressing too enthusiastically can often send bias seams into a tizzy. First, place the joined half-rectangles on your ironing surface with the darker fabric on top. Press the seam as it was sewn. This sets the stitches and helps the bias edge keep its shape. Then gently fold the upper patch out, set the iron down on the seam gently, and let the heat press the seam flat.

Skill Builder

Make a block that features a secondary pinwheel design where four blocks come together. Look for block designs that might be enhanced by this spinning effect. Add more than one round of half-rectangles to a smaller center block or fabric square and see what effects you get.

Try This!

Purchase a pack of gradated, hand-dyed fabrics to use in a lattice quilt or a mountains quilt. Arrange the colors so that they flow from left to right (for lattice) or bottom to top (for mountains). Use soft pastel colors to accent a bright print that peeks through lattice, and choose earth tones that flow into sky tones for a dramatic landscape.

FUN WITH HALF-RECTANGLES

Hassle-Free
Foundation Piecing

Foundation piecing is sweeping the quiltmaking community—and it's easy to see why. The pinpoint-accurate results this technique yields are truly spectacular. However, foundation piecing is not without its pitfalls. Sometimes fabric patches don't quite cover the area you intended, or you may have to "unsew" a patch. What then? Follow the recommendations in this chapter, and you'll be on your way to hassle-free sewing with fantastic results. You'll also have a trick or two up your sleeve to use for those times when you happen to make a mistake.

Getting Ready

The method most often used for foundation piecing is placing fabric patches underneath a foundation, then stitching on top of the foundation on a marked line. This technique yields absolute precision regardless of how narrow the pieces, how razor sharp the points, or how tricky the intersections in your pattern.

Foundations can be permanent or temporary. A permanent foundation remains part of the block; a temporary foundation is removed once the blocks are joined. Use permanent foundations for small blocks or fragile fabrics. Preshrink any fabric or interfacing that you'll use as a permanent foundation.

Use a temporary foundation material, such as freezer paper, tracing paper, or Easy Tear (a specialty product available at quilt shops), when you don't want to add an extra layer of bulk, especially when hand quilting. Paper foundations are easy to mark by needle-punching with your sewing machine, or you can purchase pre-printed paper foundations.

What You'll Need

- **Block pattern or purchased paper foundations**
- **Foundation material: tracing paper, freezer paper, Easy Tear, nonwoven interfacing, muslin, or flannel**
- **Mechanical pencil or marking pen**
- **Fabric**
- **Sewing machine**
- **Matching thread**
- **Silk pins**
- **Scissors**
- **Thread snips or embroidery scissors**
- **Rotary cutter, mat, and acrylic ruler**
- **Iron and ironing board**

Avoiding Foundation-Piecing Pitfalls

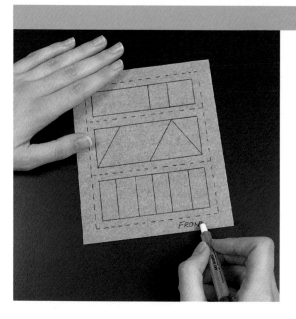

Which Side Is Up?

Whether you purchase ready-made foundations or make your own, it's easy to get confused about which side to stitch on. Remember: The side you stitch on will be the *wrong* side of your finished block. It's important to start sewing on the appropriate side of the foundation.

For instance, if you want all your schoolhouses to face the same direction, stitch all foundations from the same side. Otherwise, some houses will be reversed. **To avoid potential wrong-way blocks, mark "front" on the *sewing* side of your foundations so you won't have a mix-up.**

Tip

Freezer paper has two different textures so it's easier to tell one side from the other. Stitch on the dull side with the fabric on the shiny side.

Don't Forget Seam Allowances

Because fabric patches aren't cut to the exact size when starting out, you'll need to trim your blocks (to their *unfinished* size) after sewing. But it can be easy to forget about that outer seam allowance when trimming.

To make sure you allow for it, include a ¼-inch seam allowance on your foundation. **Use your rotary ruler and a mechanical pencil or marking pen to mark the seam allowance on all sides of the foundation before you start stitching.** You won't be likely to slip up and cut off too much fabric.

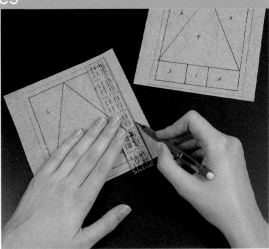

Cut Oversize Pieces

It's easier to trim off a little extra fabric than to remove and recut a skimpy patch. Cut your fabric larger than usual to ensure that you cover the areas on your foundation. **Instead of adding the usual ½ inch (¼ inch on each side) for square or rectangular areas, add ¾ inch to the finished size of the area you'll be covering.** (The finished size is what's inside the lines on the foundation.) This will give you more fabric to work with when placing your patch.

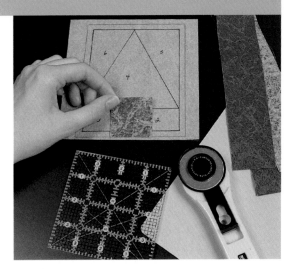

Start Off Right

1

Always position the first patch so it is *right* side up on the *wrong* side of the foundation. Pin away from the sewing lines on the foundation to hold the patch in place. Pin from the *right side* of the foundation—the front side where you'll be stitching. **Hold your foundation with the fabric away from you and with light shining through.** You should see the fabric behind the foundation covering the drawn or punched lines. Adjust as needed to leave adequate seam allowances on each side.

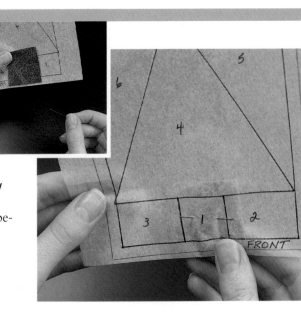

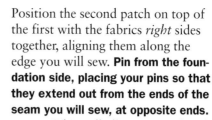

Position the second patch on top of the first with the fabrics *right* sides together, aligning them along the edge you will sew. **Pin from the foundation side, placing your pins so that they extend out from the ends of the seam you will sew, at opposite ends.**

(This will allow you to flip the patch out and check placement before it is sewn.)

Continue adding patches, always placing right sides together. The first patch is the only one that is placed right side up.

Pay Attention to Grain Line

When cutting patches for foundation-pieced blocks, make sure the outer edges of your block won't be on the bias, or the block edges will be stretchy once the foundation is removed. Even when stitched into the quilt, they'll tend to stretch.

Prevent unwanted stretching and waviness by rotary cutting patches that follow the grain line, just as you would for traditionally pieced blocks. The only difference is that they'll be cut oversize.

Watch Out for Asymmetrical Pieces

One of the trickiest parts of foundation piecing is making sure you have enough fabric to cover the shapes once the fabric has been stitched and pressed open. You're not alone if you've thought you started with a more-than-adequate piece of fabric only to find that **when opened up, the angle is off and a sliver of the area you were trying to cover is bare.**

Tip

If you have extra fabric, cut an oversize rectangle to cover an asymmetrical area, then trim it to fit after stitching.

HASSLE-FREE FOUNDATION PIECING

2

To prepare shapes other than strips, squares, or right triangles for foundation piecing, it's usually quickest and easiest to "sacrifice" one of your foundations to use for "rough-cut" templates.

Cut all the shapes needed for the pattern from the foundation. **Lay these templates right side up on the wrong side of your fabric, place your ruler on top, and cut along each edge, ⅜ inch beyond the edge of the template.**

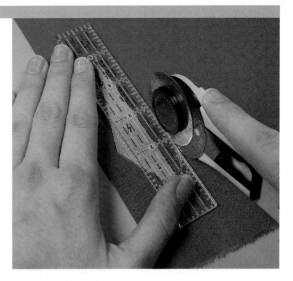

3

While it looks a little odd when positioned and ready for sewing, the patch you cut from your rough-cut template will completely fill the intended spot once it's been stitched to the foundation and pressed open. Even with template cutting, incorrect placement of the patch can still result in inadequate coverage. **To guarantee success, pin the patch in place along the stitching line, then flip it open to make sure it will cover.**

Quick Fix for a Sewing Error

If a patch doesn't cover the entire area, or if you make a mistake and the wrong side of the fabric faces up, don't try to pick out those tiny stitches. Instead, fold back the foundation and the seam allowances, leaving the incorrectly sewn patch as a single layer. **Butt your ruler up to the seam line, and cut the patch away as close as you can to the stitching.**

Then, pull away the seam allowance portion of the patch. Leave the stitching in place, cut a new patch, and sew it to the foundation.

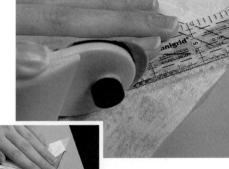

The Quilter's
Problem Solver

Removing Temporary Foundations

Problem	Solution
When removing temporary paper foundations, stitches in the sewn seams rip and pull, and the block is stretched out of shape.	Leave temporary foundations in place until the blocks have been joined together. This will help keep individual patches from pulling out of shape.
	Use as lightweight a foundation as possible. Tracing paper tears away much more easily than freezer paper.
	Use a shorter stitch length. The smaller the stitch, the closer together the perforations are and the easier it is to tear away the paper.
Excess fabric in seam allowances creates too much bulk.	After stitching each seam, place the foundation with fabric side down on a cutting mat, fold back the foundation along the line you just stitched, and trim the seam allowance to ¼ inch with your rotary cutter and ruler.

Skill Builder

If your quilt is too heavy to handle with all the extra weight of the foundations, you can reduce the weight by removing them as you go.

Once a block is surrounded on all sides, by either other blocks or sashing, its edges are stabilized. Remove the foundations from these stabilized blocks as you assemble the quilt, and you'll find that it will also reduce the stiffness and weight of the quilt, making it easier to manipulate as you sew.

Try This!

Patterns with intersecting lines, crossing lines, and inset patches cannot be pieced on a whole foundation.

It is often possible to break the block into segments, piece each segment on a foundation, and then piece the segments together to form the block. Examine your pattern to see if it can be segmented. If so, draw the pattern onto a single foundation, then cut the foundation into segments. Don't forget to add ¼ inch outside all edges of each segment for seam allowances!

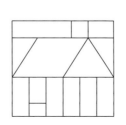 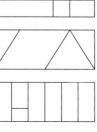

Foundations Plus!
Combining Techniques

Think of foundation piecing as another tool in your piecing repertoire. You can use foundation piecing even when your quilt isn't primarily designed for it. Use foundations to piece parts of blocks where precision and stability are difficult to achieve by other techniques, to prepare fabric to be used in pieced and appliqué designs, in constructing sashing and borders that fit exactly, or simply to stabilize tricky pieces. Explore the possibilities of foundation piecing and your quiltmaking will be faster, easier, and more precise.

Getting Ready

With some quilt projects, it's easy to see what areas can be stitched more easily by using foundation piecing. In a New York Beauty block, for instance, the sharply pointed rays are made infinitely easier by stitching the narrow points onto a foundation. Pieced Double Wedding Ring arcs are another good place to use traditional foundation piecing. But not every aspect of these familiar quilts needs to be pieced onto a foundation. The larger concave patches that these pieced arcs will be attached to are usually made of just one fabric. However, by using a single stabilizer foundation, a separate foundation for each patch in a block, you can make the marking, cutting, and even sewing of these adjoining pieces easier, too. So gather your foundation materials, including freezer paper, and get ready to make these complex quilts with intricate piecing. They'll go together more easily than you ever imagined.

What You'll Need

Fabric

Foundation material: freezer paper, tissue paper, or Easy Tear

Mechanical pencil or fabric marking pen

Scissors

Iron and ironing board

Sewing machine

Matching thread

Silk pins

Thread snips or embroidery scissors

Rotary cutter, mat, and acrylic ruler

Stabilizing Curves

Can you imagine making this New York Beauty block using templates, cutting out the long, skinny triangles, then sewing all those bias edges together, and still making sharp, precise points? **Use foundations in several ways to help ensure nice, sharp points and smooth curves in this block.** First you'll need a printed pattern to work from, or if you prefer, you can draft your own.

2

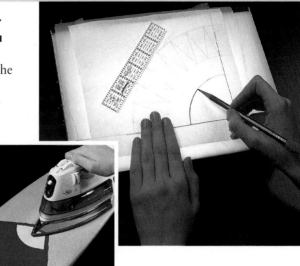

Make a single foundation of freezer paper to help stabilize fabric as you draw curves. Trace your pattern onto freezer paper so it is the *finished size*, without seam allowances. **Cut the finished size foundation and press it (shiny side down) onto the *wrong* side of the fabric.** Once pressed in place, the freezer paper holds the fabric taut as you use a pencil or fabric marking pen to draw along its edge to mark the curved stitching line. Without the foundation, the fabric stretches and pulls when you draw.

Tip

If you don't have a light box, tape your pattern and freezer paper to a sunny window and trace the shape.

3

Draw around the edge of the freezer paper foundation with a sharp pencil. The foundation will prevent drag as you mark.

Cut around the foundation, adding a ¼-inch seam allowance as you cut. The foundation prevents distortion as you cut out the patch. Remove the foundation before piecing, and save it to mark additional pieces until it won't press onto the fabric anymore.

If your pattern has an additional arc, such as the red piece in the sample on page 75, make a freezer paper foundation, mark, and cut it in the same manner.

Tip

Draw the seam allowance around your foundation if you aren't comfortable eyeballing ¼ inch while cutting.

4

Long, narrow repetitive points are well suited to piecing on a foundation. **Piece the circular arc portions of the New York Beauty on marked foundations.** The points will be sharp, the bias edges will be stable, and you will have an accurate guide for joining the segment to other pieces of the block. This also works well for the pieced arcs of a Double Wedding Ring.

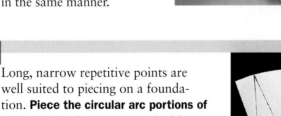

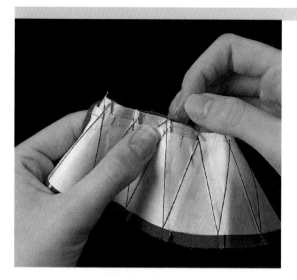

If your pattern has multipart arcs as the sample does, stitch the solid fabric pieces together first, matching them along the drawn seam lines. **Then pin the foundation-pieced arc to the piece(s) cut with the single stabilizer foundation, matching the edge of the foundation to the drawn seam line.** To make sure you have a smooth, even curve, pin the ends, then the center, then midway between the center and each end. Add more pins for larger pieces. Sew the pieces together slowly and carefully, easing the curve as you go.

Foundations for Sashing and Borders

When sashing is stitched to a block or a row of blocks, the weight of the blocks can pull the sashing out of shape. **To stabilize narrow sashing or a single-fabric border while it is being stitched, make a single stabilizer foundation from freezer paper.** Cut freezer paper to the *finished* size of the sashing, press onto the fabric, and use a rotary cutter and ruler to add ¼-inch seam allowances on all edges. Line up the edge of the single foundation with the stitching line of the blocks for a stable, consistent sash or border.

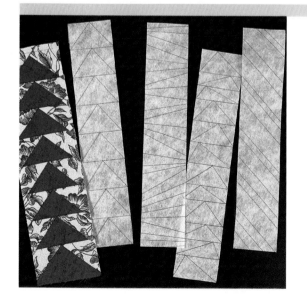

Pieced sashing may be just what you need to perk up your quilt. Piece sashing on a temporary foundation, and it will be exactly the size you need and won't stretch out of shape.

Cut the foundation to the exact finished size of your sashing, and divide it into equal segments by measuring or folding. With a sharp pencil, draw the design or pattern on the foundation. Mark for straight strips, diagonal strips, triangles, Flying Geese, random Flying Geese, or anything else that strikes your fancy. Stitch the sashing to your quilt blocks using the edge of the foundation as a guide.

3

Pieced borders are notoriously stretchy, even when pieced with the proper grain orientation. For maximum control and a perfect fit, piece borders on foundations. Many triangle and strip designs can be pieced completely on one foundation. Other designs may need to be pieced in segments or with some single foundation elements. **The border is easiest to sew in place when the foundation is cut to the finished width, with the fabric extending ¼ inch beyond all sides;** this way, you won't have to sew through the foundation when joining the border to the quilt top.

Using Foundations with Appliqué

Foundation-Pieced Appliqués

Use a temporary foundation to stabilize a pieced pattern, such as a Wheel of Fortune or Dresden Plate, that will be appliquéd to a background. The appliqué will then lie flat on the background. If you plan to cut away the background fabric under the appliqué after stitching, leave the foundation on as a guide for basting the edges or for needle-turn appliqué. If you leave the background whole, stay stitch the edge and remove the foundation before appliquéing.

Foundation-Pieced Backgrounds

A varied background adds interest to many appliqué shapes. Crazy piecing is a fun way to use up scraps of fabric and at the same time makes an interesting background. Other types of blocks can be used, too, such as a Square within a Square, Log Cabin, and others. The key is to keep fabric contrast subtle so the appliqué can take center stage. **Use a temporary foundation to piece a background, then remove the foundation before appliquéing the shape on top.** Stay stitch ⅛ inch from the outer edges of the pieced block to stabilize it before removing the foundation.

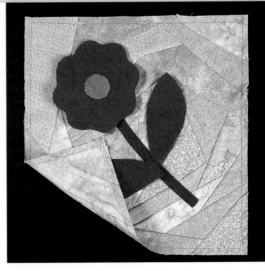

The Quilter's
Problem Solver

Bulky Seam Intersections

Problem

When stitching foundation-pieced units together, the bulk makes matching points slip out of alignment as you sew.

Solution

Sometimes the added bulk of too many layers of paper or other foundation material can be too much for your sewing machine to handle. For assembling sections of a pieced block, you can tear away the seam allowance part of the foundation before sewing the various sections together. For sashings and borders, sometimes it's easier to start with a foundation that is cut to the finished size and doesn't include seam allowances. (It will be easier to remove in the end, too!)

Transfer your foundation-piecing skills to garment making!

If you are making a quilted garment using foundation piecing and plan to add batting, you will probably want a temporary foundation that will not add additional bulk. This is doubly true if your garment will be hand-quilted.

If a finishing lining but no batting will be added before quilting, a permanent foundation may help your jacket or vest to hang better, and it will provide some definition and dimension for the quilting. If the garment is made of a lightweight silk or wool, a foundation of batiste would provide support without changing the drape of the fabric. For cotton or heavier wool garments, you can use muslin or flannel.

Try This!

Choose the stitch length on your sewing machine according to the technique and foundation material being used.

To avoid distortion when removing temporary foundations, use a short stitch (15 to 18 stitches per inch on a standard machine or 1.5 to 1.75 on a metric machine). Use a regular stitch length when using permanent foundations, single foundation piecing, or conventional piecing without a temporary foundation.

Foundation Piecing:
Beyond the Lines

Foundation piecing seems to grow in popularity by leaps and bounds. Like a coloring book or a paint-by-number set, preprinted foundations supply quilters with a range of patterns. You'll be able to make even the most intricate blocks without any of the difficulties of standard piecing. No need to stick to the given lines, though! Instead, use your imagination to venture beyond them with a change or two that makes the design more interesting and uniquely yours.

Getting Ready

This chapter features Foundation by the Yard, a product from Benartex, designed by quilter Sharon Hultgren. You can adapt the technique to any preprinted foundation.

Foundation by the Yard is preprinted muslin. Each panel includes blocks for the quilt, design ideas, fabric requirements, and instructions for preparing and using the panels for foundation piecing. The fabric foundations are permanent: They stay in your quilt after you're done piecing.

Choose a panel of Foundation by the Yard and press it only enough to remove large creases. (Steaming the panel may distort the printed lines.) If you prewash the panel, make sure you block the lines into position again. Cut the blocks (or half-blocks) apart. Select your fabrics according to the directions, and be sure you have enough contrast in your colors to accentuate the patterns. Follow the directions on the panels for assembly, and read the steps below for ideas to vary the basic design.

What You'll Need

Panels of Foundation by the Yard by Benartex (or other preprinted foundation patterns)

Prewashed, pressed fabric as indicated on each panel, and additional fabrics as desired

Hard-lead pencil

Rotary cutter, mat, and acrylic rulers

Silk pins

Sewing machine

Template plastic

Hunter's Star with an Accent

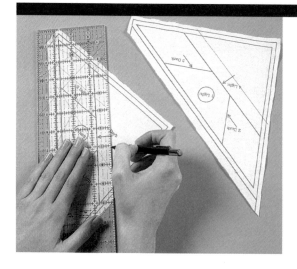

The Hunter's Star block can be arranged and rearranged to create fun variations. You can also add design elements to the block as an accent or to create a secondary design.

To recreate the block variation shown on the opposite page (designed by Sharon Hultgren), you'll need to add just one line to each unit that makes up one-quarter of a block. **Draw a pencil line in the number 4 areas, parallel to and ¾ inch from the existing diagonal line.**

Tip

When adding lines to printed blocks, do it with a hard-lead pencil so the marks won't smudge or bleed through the fabrics when you press.

2

Piece areas 1, 2, and 3 as directed on the foundations, using a *longer* stitch length than normal. A longer stitch length prevents puckers and makes it easier to sew over the silk pins and rip out the occasional mistake. Cut 1¼ inch-wide strips of the accent fabric (choose a color that contrasts with both your lights and your darks), and **place one right side down along the area 4 line. You may want to pin the fabric in place.** Sew along the line, then press the fabric into area 4.

3

Tip

If desired, stay stitch around the unit to keep the edges secure.

Complete the unit by adding your area 4 fabric. Press and trim to the printed dashed line on the foundation. **Compare the look of the altered triangle unit to one that does not have the accent strip added.** For each block, make two triangular units, reversing the main colors, and sew together to form a square. When these blocks are assembled, **the strips of accent-color fabric come together to create nicely mitered square frames.**

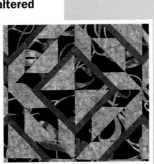

Crazy for You with a Window

1

Tip

Label the side that was facing down as you traced, "Front," so you'll know how to position and cut a printed fabric for the window.

The Crazy for You blocks are perfect for playful quiltmaking. One fun way to vary the basic panel is to combine the first three areas into one piece and use a conversation print in the block's center "window."

Lay template plastic on the center of a Crazy for You block, and trace ¼ inch outside the lines that enclose areas 1, 2, and 3. Cut out the template and **lay it on your fabric, centering a motif.** Trace around the template. In this way, cut out as many motifs as you need.

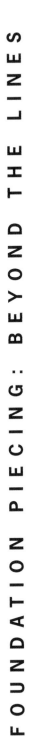

Pin the conversation print motif right side up on the wrong (unprinted) side of the foundation. It should cover the first three sections of the block. Begin the regular piecing with the number 4 area. **Place a strip of fabric right side down on the wrong side of the Foundation by the Yard, aligning it with the edge of the center fabric along the area 4 line. Pin to secure.** Sew along the printed lines, **adding more strips until your block is completed.**

Tip

Consider incorporating specialty fabrics such as lace and lightweight silk into your block. The foundation will keep it stabilized.

Flying Geese Pinwheels

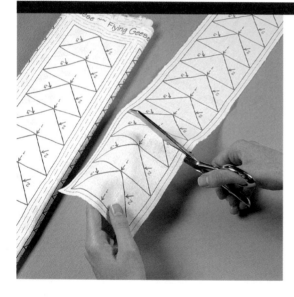

To make "flying pinwheels" from the Foundation by the Yard Flying Geese panel, a design created by Pam Hultgren-Klein, cut one strip of large flying geese from the panel. **Cut the strip into pairs of geese, cutting through the middle of the geese on either side.**

Tip

Measure to see if your foundation blocks are printed straight on the fabric. If not, block them into shape before starting to sew fabric pieces onto them.

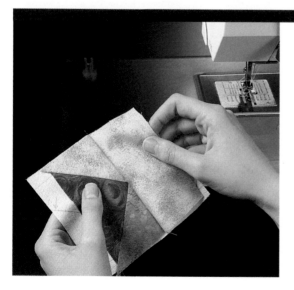

Piece the bottom goose as usual (reading the numbers normally and following them chronologically), using a dark fabric for area 1, a light-colored fabric for area 2, and a medium fabric for area 3. **For the top goose, cover areas 1, 2, and 3 with one rectangle of the same light fabric (2½ × 4½ inches), ignoring the printed lines.** Be sure to trim the seam allowances of the darker fabrics so that they don't shadow through.

Tip

Check to make sure the unused lines on the foundation won't show through your light-colored fabric.

FOUNDATION PIECING: BEYOND THE LINES

3

Join four units together with the dark patches at the center to make a finished Pinwheel block. Press the seam allowances open between pinwheel units to help match the center of the block and to minimize bulk.

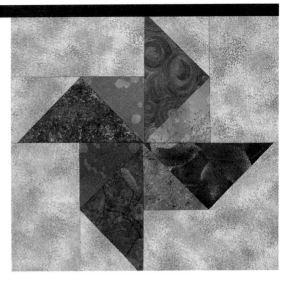

Square-by-Square Snail's Trail

1

Turn a panel of Square by Square into a wonderful Snail's Trail quilt with another of Sharon Hultgren's variations. All you have to do is add a small four patch to the center of the block.

Using a lead pencil, measure and mark the midpoint of each side of the center square—$1\frac{3}{8}$ inches from each corner. **Connect these midpoints to draw a scant 2-inch square.**

2

Create a four-patch unit for the center: First, sew a light- and a dark-colored $1\frac{1}{2}$-inch-wide strip together into a strip set. Press seam allowances toward the darker strip. Cut the strip set crosswise into $1\frac{1}{2}$-inch-wide segments, and sew the segments into four-patch units. Press. (See the Four Patch Block on page 34 for details.) **Working on the reverse side of the foundation, position the four-patch unit carefully over the drawn center square.** To help promote accurate placement, pin through both the four-patch and foundation block centers.

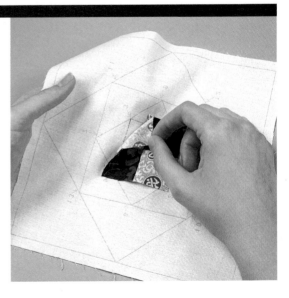

Cut additional strips from your light- and dark-colored fabrics to sew around the center four-patch unit. Cut strips at least ½ inch wider than the areas you'll be covering.

Tip

Layer your light and dark fabrics and cut them together to save time.

Pin strips around the center four patch. To maintain the pattern, use increasingly wider strips of fabric for each round, and follow the light and dark specifications, as indicated by the color placement provided with the Foundation by the Yard product. Press and trim each piece after it is added.

Square up the blocks, trimming ¼ inch beyond the solid line. **Arrange the blocks so that the Snail's Trail pattern is established.**

FOUNDATION PIECING: BEYOND THE LINES

Free-Form
Strip-Pieced Yardage

Y ou're going to love this fresh, fun technique that utilizes simple strip-pieced sections to give the illusion of complex composition. All you have to do is cut strips, sew them together, then cut those resulting strip sets into more strips, sewing them together in any way you desire. You can plan your fabric choices and placements carefully, or go random and see what happens—either way, you'll be amazed how your project grows and blossoms into a one-of-a-kind quilt.

Getting Ready

Select fabrics in your desired colors, choosing a variety of print scales, values, textures, and intensities. The intended size of your completed project and the number of fabrics you want to include will determine how much fabric you choose or purchase, but five different fabrics in either fat quarters or ¼ yard cuts would be sufficient for most wall hangings. Use ½ yard of fabric if you decide to cut it on the bias rather than on the crosswise straight grain. Many fabrics have a very different look when cut this way! Fold the fabrics and overlap them on a work surface so just a portion of each is visible. Play with the arrangement of fabrics until you are pleased with the range, the selection, and the way the fabrics work together.

Note: In order to present techniques within the framework of the step-by-step photographs that follow, we show a relatively small piece of yardage being made. Using the same techniques but cutting strips from the full width of your fabric, you can make strip-pieced yardage 40 inches square, or as large as you need.

What You'll Need

- **Prewashed, pressed fabrics**
- **Rotary cutter, mat, and acrylic ruler**
- **Sewing machine**
- **Walking-foot attachment or even-feed feature**
- **Iron and ironing board**
- **Batting**
- **Backing fabric**
- **Chalk pencil**
- **Pins**

Making the Yardage

Cut strips of varying widths from your selected group of fabrics. Generally, widths should range between 2 inches and 4 inches. **Arrange your cut strips on a work surface.** Keep strips cut from each fabric together, arranged from narrowest to widest. You'll find this helps with both easy identification and access to the strips as you plan your arrangement and sew.

Tip

Use an expanding wooden drying rack to hang your strips. Place each fabric on a separate rod, arranged from narrowest to widest.

2

To begin piecing, select the strips
you want to use. Stack the strips in
order, with the first (left-hand) strip
on the top of the stack and the last
(right-hand) strip on the bottom.
Pick up the top two strips from your
pile. **Place the second strip on top of
the first strip, right sides together,
and sew the two strips together, using a ¼-inch seam
allowance.** Use a stitch length
of 12 to 14 stitches per inch,
so that there's less chance of
stitches coming loose when
the yardage is cut. **From the
right side, finger press the
sewn seam to one side.**

3

Pick up the third strip from your pile
and place it on top of the second
strip, with right sides together.
Sew the strips as you did before,
unfold the top strip, and working
from the right side, finger press the
seam flat. Press seams all in one
direction. Repeat for all remaining strips.

**Press the entire string-pieced
yardage on the wrong side.** It's
best to move your iron perpendicular to the seams, rather
than parallel to them, to avoid
distortion. Repeat to make as
many strip sets as you wish.

4

To cut your strip set into slices, lay it
flat on a cutting mat. Make a straight-
ening cut on one end, and rotate your
cutting mat (not your strip set). **For
slices perpendicular to your seams,
align a horizontal line on your ruler
with a seam line and cut slices to the
desired width.** Align the ruler
with a seam each time you
cut a slice.

**If you want to cut your strip
set on the bias, align the
45 degree angle line on your
ruler with a seam line to
make your cuts.**

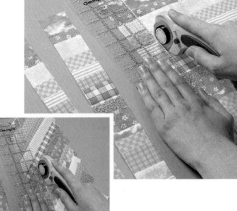

Blocks and Patches from Your Yardage

Generally, you can use your strip-pieced yardage as regular yardage, and cut blocks or large patches from them. Avoid cutting too close to the seam lines; you don't want the bulk of seam allowances within the newly created seam allowances or too-thin slivers of a fabric that might look like a mistake. **Try combining straight-cut sections with bias-cut ones for a fresh twist on even the simplest of One Patch patterns.**

Tip

Machine baste the edges of your patches or blocks to prevent small pieces from coming unsewn.

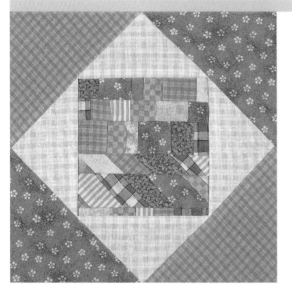

Your strip-pieced yardage is a one-of-a-kind fabric; take advantage of its unique appeal. **Cut large patches from your strip-pieced yardage, and give them a central role to play in a traditional patchwork block.** Frame your strip-pieced patches with contrasting or coordinating plain patches.

Quick Quilts and Quilted Backgrounds

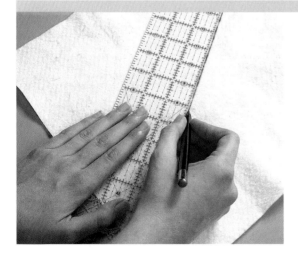

Here's a fun, quick way to put a small strip-pieced quilt together, assembling and quilting all at once. Cut batting and backing at least 2 inches larger all around than the desired finished quilt. If you foresee adding quilting around appliqués or free-motion quilting, set the backing aside and work with only the batting for now. Otherwise, layer the batting on top of the backing. **Use a chalk pencil or other soft marking tool to draw a straight line across the center of the batting in the direction you wish your strips to lie.**

FREE-FORM STRIP-PIECED YARDAGE

Tip

Use a walking-foot attachment or the even-feed feature on your sewing machine to help keep all the layers properly aligned.

2

Decide on the order for your slices. Since you are starting in the middle, you will have one stack of slices that will fill the first half of the batting, and a second stack for the second half. Stack them as you did in Step 2 on page 88, with the slice you will place first (in the center of your quilt) on the top of your first stack. **Pin the first slice right side up on the batting, aligning one long edge with your drawn line.** Position the second slice in your stack right side down on the first slice, with raw edges even. **Sew through all layers, using a ¼-inch seam allowance.**

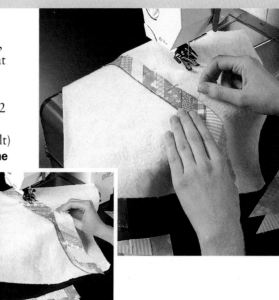

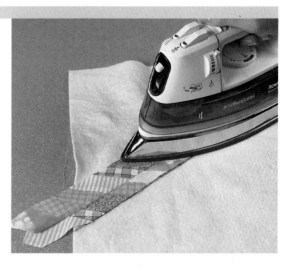

3

Remove the quilt from the machine. **Unfold the second slice, press the seam flat, then pin it in place.** This ensures straight seam lines in a piece using long slices. Continue adding strips in this manner, pressing after each slice is added, until you reach the end of the first side.

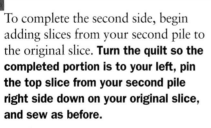

4

To complete the second side, begin adding slices from your second pile to the original slice. **Turn the quilt so the completed portion is to your left, pin the top slice from your second pile right side down on your original slice, and sew as before.**

Continue adding and pressing slices until the background is completed. **Add appliqués, if desired,** plus a backing if you have not done so. Quilt around the appliqués or as desired to secure the layers. Trim the edges, and finish with a binding.

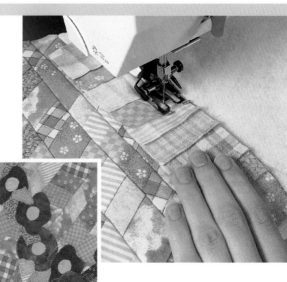

The Quilter's
Problem Solver

Avoiding Distortion

Problem	Solution
The strips in my strip-pieced yardage all curve to the left.	The tension on your top thread is too tight. Loosen the top tension slightly, or tighten the bobbin tension until you have a balanced stitch.
The strips all curve to the right.	The tension on the bobbin is too tight. Increase the top tension or loosen the bobbin tension slightly until you have a balanced stitch.
The tension is balanced, but the strip-pieced yardage still curves.	Careful pressing will help ensure that your seams lie flat and straight. Always press with the iron crossing the seam, not moving along it, to prevent distortion. Press gently but firmly, never dragging the iron, which can pull the fabric out of shape.
The strip-pieced yardage "scallops" or appears wavy.	Your tension is too tight (even if balanced). Loosen the tension. Also, try pressing each seam as it is sewn, then unfolding the strip to press it out. This helps ease out any puckers.

Skill Builder

If you just can't get your fabrics to work together, try one of these tips:

• Use a multicolor print between two prints that clash. A print that contains both colors will "bridge the gap."

• Can't find a good color match among your fabrics? Diversify! The more fabrics in the mix, and the more shades of your dominant color, the more interesting the end result will be.

• Remove any fabrics that stand out too much. Close your eyes, then blink three times at your arrangement. Take out the fabric you "see" when your eyes are closed.

Try This!

Free-form strip-pieced yardage makes very interesting backgrounds for appliqué designs and other graphic elements. When you just can't find a background fabric that has enough interest, make your own by combining different shades, textures, and scales of neutral fabrics. Want a really riotous background for your appliqué quilt? Cut your strip-pieced yardage into random shapes and crazy piece them together!

Playing with
String Piecing

String piecing began as the ultimate scrap technique. It was a way for quilters of the past to create warm, beautiful patchwork from all those long, skinny strips and leftovers from dressmaking and quilting projects. It was like getting something from nothing—the pioneers' version of recycling! Today this old favorite has been reborn as a fun and freeing way to use all of our wildest fabrics to make bright, exuberant quilts that sizzle with energy.

Getting Ready

String piecing is done on a foundation to stabilize the scraps, which often have bias edges or are so thin they cannot hold their own shape. The foundation can be a lightweight fabric, such as muslin or broadcloth. Traditionally, these quilts were tied as comforters, rather than quilted, since the foundation adds another layer of thickness that makes it difficult to quilt by hand. If you prefer to hand quilt, piece your string blocks on a temporary foundation of lightweight paper, which will be torn away when the quilt top is completed. Unprinted newsprint works very well, as does examining table paper (available at medical supply stores), which is inexpensive and tears away easily. Use any fabrics you have for string piecing—the sky's the limit. Beginners may want to stick to 100 percent cottons for easier sewing, but don't overlook other fabrics to add texture and dimension to your work.

What You'll Need

Variety of fabric strings and other odd-size scraps

Foundation material: muslin, broadcloth, or lightweight paper

Rotary cutter, mat, and acrylic ruler

Sewing machine

Neutral color cotton thread

Iron and ironing board

Basic Diagonal String Block

1

Select fabrics to cut strings from, and sort through your existing scraps to add to your choices. The more colors and types of prints you include, the better. You'll be amazed at how different they look cut into smaller pieces. **Vary the width of the strips from 1½ to 4 inches; the edges do not have to be parallel and are more interesting if they taper.** Cut foundations from fabric or paper. Remember to cut them ½ inch larger than the block size you're making (for example, cut 8½ inches square for an 8-inch-square finished block).

Tip

Look beyond small prints and calicoes—try cutting strings from stripes, plaids, and large-scale, splashy prints.

2

Tip

Try to vary the colors, prints, and widths of the strings as you add them.

To begin a basic block, pick a long string and place it, right side up, diagonally across the foundation square, from corner to corner. Choose a second string, and place it on top of the first string, with right sides together and edges even. **Pin in place if desired, and sew through all three layers to attach both strings to the foundation, using a ¼-inch seam allowance.** Flip the second string right side up; press. Continue to add strings until the foundation is covered. **Finger press or iron each string as you add it.**

3

Tip

When joining string-pieced blocks, press the block seams open to alleviate bulk where seams cross.

When the block is finished, press it one more time, and lay it pieced side down on your cutting mat. **Position the ruler on the block, aligning the edge of the ruler with the raw edges of the foundation. With the rotary cutter, trim off all the excess fabric extending beyond the edges of the foundation.** Repeat on all remaining sides.

String-Piecing Variations

1

For a fanlike look, **place each string so that the narrow, tapered end is always toward one corner.** Your strings will splay out, and you can do a lot of creative designing with sunbursts and floral themes.

If you have a lot of shorter strings that don't extend all the way from one side or corner of the foundation to the other, you can still incorporate them into your design. Start in one corner, sewing the strings to the foundation. Cover one side of the foundation completely. **Then, fill in any gap left with a larger scrap, sewn to cover the "hole" that the other strings left.**

For an effective design with half the work, **use a print as your foundation.** To make this Roman Stripes block, start with one string, placing it on the foundation print, with right sides together. (The print fabric will act as your foundation and also your first "string.") **Cover only half the square with strings, letting your print fabric foundation show on the other half.**

Tip

You'll enjoy machine quilting with this method; it's not well suited for hand quilting.

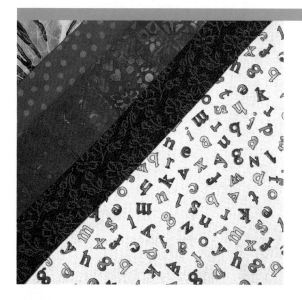

This is a fun way to use up all the scraps you have at the end of your sewing session (you know, the ones that are just a little too big to throw away). **Make a small "End of the Day" quilt** (as Diane Rode Schneck likes to call it). Often, the results of such quick recycling efforts come out better than the carefully planned quilts we slave over! Strip-pieced segments and crazy piecing—or whatever strikes the quiltmaker's fancy—all come into play in this quilt. Sashing and corner squares impose just the right amount of order in assembling these blocks.

PLAYING WITH STRING PIECING

Sherlock on the Block:
Clues for Cutting & Piecing

I t's elementary, dear quilter. You, too, can figure out how to put together many of those quilts you've admired at shows, in books, or in magazines. While at first they may appear too complicated to tackle, the solutions come from looking at them from a fresh perspective. With a little practice, you'll be a super sleuth at deciphering blocks and reducing them to small units that are easy to rotary cut, speed piece, and assemble into quilts.

Getting Ready

What You'll Need

Quilting books, magazines, and photos of quilts

Graph paper or a computer drawing program

Sharp pencil

Ruler

Calculator

One of the best ways to analyze quilt blocks is to view as many different blocks as possible. Visit a quilt show, and browse through your quilting magazines and books. Draft some of the examples you see in different sizes. A wonderful aspect of rotary cutting is that it eliminates templates, but that doesn't mean you should eliminate drafting from your repertoire. Drawing blocks on paper or on the computer is one of the best ways to become familiar with them. Experiment with the blocks shown in this chapter and with as many others as you can find. In no time you'll be in the habit of looking at blocks in a whole new light, deconstructing them into subunits and specific shapes, and putting them back together with ease.

Block Detective

The Case of the Grid

Most quilt blocks fall into categories that describe how their patches are arranged. **Terms like One Patch, Four Patch, and Nine Patch all describe the** *grid* **upon which each block is based.** A one-patch quilt contains repeats of just one shape. Four-patch blocks have an initial gridwork of four equal units, two across and two down. Nine-patch blocks are composed of nine equal units (3×3). A designation like 5×5 or 7×7 (Five Patch and Seven Patch) refers to the number of units in each horizontal and vertical row, rather than the number of units in the grid.

Keep It Simple

Once you analyze a block's basic grid, it's easy to determine a finished size that can be quickly and accurately cut with rotary equipment. It would be difficult to cut pieces for a 9-inch block as drafted here because when we fit the five-across and five-down grid into the 9-inch space, the dimensions for each unit aren't on a rotary ruler: $9 \div 5 = 1.8$ inches. A 10-inch block would work much better: $10 \div 5 = 2$ inches for each unit in the grid. In general, try to find a size that will allow you to work in ¼-inch increments.

Sizing Up . . . or Down

Another easy way to establish block size is to determine the number of units in the block first, then decide how large you want each unit to be. Multiply the unit dimension by the number of units across and down the grid to calculate the finished block size. **Increase or decrease the per-unit size until you're satisfied with the size of the finished block.**

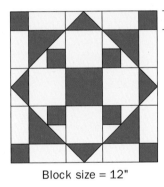

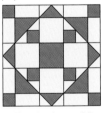

Unit size = 1½"

Unit size = 1"

Block size = 12"

Block size = 8"

Pay Attention to the Little Guys

If your block has units that are subdivided, or pieced, you'll need to consider those when determining a finished block size. The units in a simple Nine Patch block can be any size marked on a rotary ruler because each unit is made from a single piece of fabric. **But in a Double Nine Patch, five of the units contain smaller Nine Patch blocks.** If each large square is 4 inches, it will be difficult to rotary cut the small units ($4 \div 3 = 1.333$). A 3¾-inch square will work; it results in a finished size of 1¼ inch for the small units. This is easily measured with a rotary ruler.

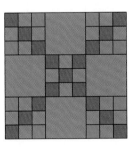

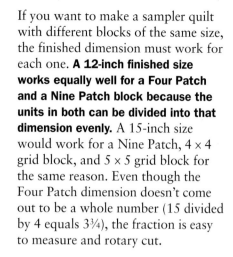

The Sampler Challenge

If you want to make a sampler quilt with different blocks of the same size, the finished dimension must work for each one. **A 12-inch finished size works equally well for a Four Patch and a Nine Patch block because the units in both can be divided into that dimension evenly.** A 15-inch size would work for a Nine Patch, 4 × 4 grid block, and 5 × 5 grid block for the same reason. Even though the Four Patch dimension doesn't come out to be a whole number (15 divided by 4 equals 3¾), the fraction is easy to measure and rotary cut.

Framed!

When it becomes too difficult to find a common size for all the blocks you want to include in a sampler quilt, **add sashing, or a frame, around smaller blocks to compensate for the difference.** To find the width to cut your framing fabric, subtract the finished size of a small block from the finished size of the largest block. Divide the result by 2 and add ½ inch. Sew two strips of this width to opposite sides of the unfinished *small* block, then to the remaining sides. Both blocks should now be the same size.

Grain Considerations

The Cutting Edge

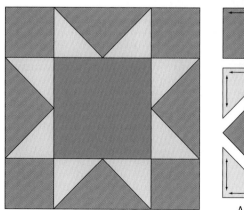

Arrows indicate straight grain

For maximum stability, the outer edges of a block should always be on the straight grain. If the stretchy bias is on the outer edge of a block, this edge is likely to become distorted with handling and be more difficult to sew to other blocks or lattice. Squares and rectangles are easy to cut on the straight grain. A triangle is an example of a patch that always has at least one bias edge. **These stretchy edges should be placed on the interior of the block,** sewn to a straight-grain edge when possible, to help stabilize them.

CLUES FOR CUTTING & PIECING

99

Half- versus Quarter-Square Triangle

A right triangle is a basic shape in quiltmaking; it is most often cut from a square with sides cut along the straight grain. **If you want the short sides of a right triangle to be straight grain, start with a square, and cut it in half diagonally to make two half-square triangles.** If the long side of the triangle will be placed on the perimeter of the block, you'll want these to be along the straight grain. Start with a square again, but **cut the square in half along both diagonals to produce four quarter-square triangles.**

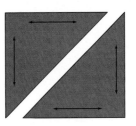 

Half-square triangles

Quarter-square triangles

Case Studies

Jacob's Ladder Block

At first glance, the traditional Jacob's Ladder block may appear complicated, but a closer look reveals how simple it really is. All you have is a Nine Patch design, even though each of its nine "patches" have been subdivided. **Five of the nine units in the grid are simple Four Patch blocks, which can be strip-pieced.** Refer to "Build Your Strip-Piecing Skills" on page 32. **The remaining four units are triangle squares.** See "Once Upon a Triangle Square" on page 46.

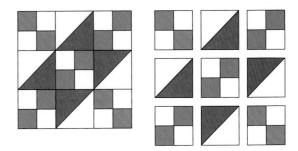

Eight-Pointed Star Block

When you have unusual shapes such as diamonds, their dimensions usually determine the sizes for other pieces. **Most often, the length of a side on these shapes is the basis for all other cutting.** This Eight-Pointed Star is assembled with 45 degree diamonds (see page 37). The diamond's finished leg length determines the finished size of each corner square. The remaining pieces are quarter-square triangles, with long, straight-grain edges at the perimeter of the block. Their short sides are equal in length to the diamond's leg.

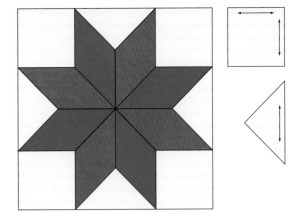

Bachelor's Puzzle Block

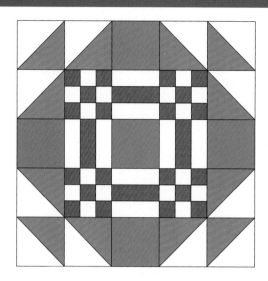

The traditional Bachelor's Puzzle block is a 5 x 5 grid, with 25 equal units arranged 5 across and 5 down. The units are composed of plain squares, triangle squares, and two different types of units based on a 3 × 3 grid. One is a checkerboard Nine Patch; the other contains three striped rows.

Tip

To determine overall block size, first determine the size of the Nine Patch units.

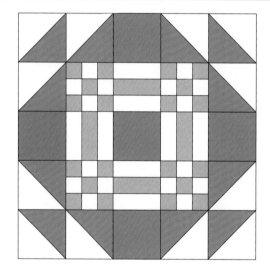

Quick piece the 12 triangle squares that are arranged at the corners of the block using your favorite technique. Between the triangle squares, at the center of each outside row, is a simple square. Cut these squares quickly and easily from strips of fabric.

The Nine Patch and striped units are both pieced using the same two strip sets. **The segments that form the top and bottom rows of the Nine Patch units are cut from a "dark-light-dark" strip set; the center row contains segments cut from a "light-dark-light" strip set. The striped units are longer segments cut from the same light-dark-light strip set.**

Fast, Faux
Mini Quilts

*W*ouldn't you love to make a miniature quilt—one with all the appeal of a tiny textile treasure, but none of the fussy, time-consuming, and eye-straining assembling of tiny patches or super-narrow multiple borders? With our tricks, you'll dash off little quilts that look like you've spent hours and hours working on them. Astonished friends are sure to ask, "How did you ever do it?"

Getting Ready

Read through the steps in this chapter to become familiar with the shortcut techniques. Then visit a fabric store, and take your time browsing through the aisles. Pull out the fabrics for a better view—sometimes just looking at the end of the bolt isn't enough. Keep an eye out for even or uneven stripes and checkerboards, both tiny scale and oversize, two-tone or multicolor. Look for any fabric with a good, small-scale geometric pattern, a quilt block in miniature, even a printed pillow panel with a patchwork design. Many fabrics offer small motifs—great for "pretend" appliqué blocks. When you get home, pull out your cutting equipment and try one of the little projects described here. Experiment with striped fabric to simulate strip sets for many of the full-scale ideas throughout this book. In next to no time, you'll be ready to convert many of your favorite blocks into marvelous miniatures.

Small-Scale Sensations

Quilting Makes It a Quilt

The secret behind these shortcut minis is the use of small- or medium-scale prints to simulate meticulously worked patchwork and appliqué. **To make the illusion more believable, always add quilting.** Use flannel or very thin batting if you want a filler. Hand or machine quilt between stripes or color areas to simulate stitching in the ditches of seams. For faux appliqué, quilt around a printed motif, as you would an appliquéd shape. With fine stitches, this effort lends much more credibility to the sense that tiny handwork has taken place.

 Tip

Use clear nylon thread to give your piece the dimensionality of quilting without noticeable stitches.

FAST, FAUX MINI QUILTS

Mini Album Quilt

Many prints feature well-spaced, small motifs. Printed pillow panels often contain small-scale images of pieced blocks. **Watch for fabrics that contain miniaturized medallions, pictures of seed packets, feed sack images, reprints of advertising items, or other pictorial scenes in small, contained areas.** Cut these motifs into individual printed "blocks," leaving ¼-inch seam allowances all around. To enhance the pieced look, quilt along all of the printed lines. Incorporate small plaids, gingham, and tiny, overall prints, keeping in scale with the motifs.

Stripes in Place of Strip Sets

Amish Bars

To make a quick and easy Amish Bars quilt, substitute a multicolor striped print for a strip set made from narrow pieces of fabric. Even if this results in a quilt top that is slightly off grain, it will have a true "pieced" look. Cut the edges ¼ inch beyond the outer stripes, so that seams on those edges will fall on a printed line rather than within a stripe. Consider quilting between the printed stripes to create the illusion of piecing with a traditional look.

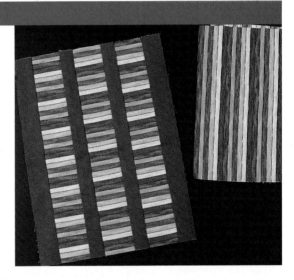

Rail Fence or Basketweave

To simulate a Rail Fence or Basketweave pattern, cut strips from an even stripe. **Cut squares from the strips, then arrange them so that the direction of the stripe alternates from patch to patch.** Machine quilt a row of stitching between the stripes in each patch.

More Fun with Stripes and Prints

Quick Nine Patch

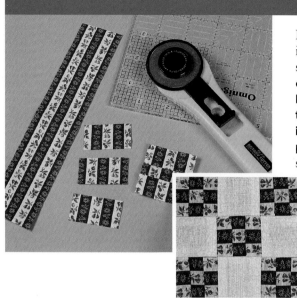

Find an evenly striped fabric, and use it as a substitute for strip sets. Cut the stripes, adding ¼ inch beyond the outer stripes. **For a shortcut Nine Patch block, cut segments across three stripes of a two-tone fabric: two identical, and one with the color placements switched.** Center the single segment between two identical segments; join these pieces, taking care to match the divisions between colors. Assemble the Nine Patch blocks in any setting you like. **Alternate plain blocks speed up the process.**

Simulated Strings

For a string-quilt look, use a fabric with uneven stripes. Cut out squares, triangles, or other shapes, and re-assemble so that the stripes do not match. Try cutting off grain for a more random look to your "strings." To stabilize these off-grain pieces, use lightweight, fusible interfacing or a temporary foundation (see "Hassle-Free Foundation Piecing" on page 68).

Tip

Cut a "window" out of cardboard to preview your fabric before cutting.

Contained Crazy Quilt

For a contained crazy quilt, select a fabric with angular, abstract areas of color. Position a window template over the fabric so you can "audition" possible patches before marking and rotary-cutting patches. Alternate these wild patches with those cut from solid or, at least, quiet fabrics, so you avoid a look that's too crazy!

FAST, FAUX MINI QUILTS

Faux Half-Square Triangles

To obtain squares that seem to be made up of two contrasting-color half-square triangles, make a square template, and center it on point over two stripes. Trace the squares, and cut with a rotary cutter. Arrange the squares in blocks such as Pinwheels or Flying Geese. See "Once Upon a Triangle Square" on page 46 for more ideas. Use lightweight fusible interfacing on the back if you have trouble with bias edges stretching.

Checkerboard Options

Baskets

Use a large check to make a quick tiny "basket block." Cut out a rectangular portion containing half a check-square (the bowl of the basket), one-quarter of the check square diagonally below it (the base of the basket) plus ¼-inch seam allowances all around. For the handle, stabilize a piece of muslin or other coordinating fabric with interfacing or a tear-away backing, then machine satin stitch a half-circle on top. **Sew these two pieces together to complete your basket.**

Lattice

To make a striking lattice that simulates pieced squares on point, use a woven check fabric. Back it with very light fusible interfacing so the bias edges won't stretch. **Cut along a diagonal row of squares,** adding ¼ inch beyond points for seam allowances. **Use the resulting strips for bars or borders, sashing, and insets.**

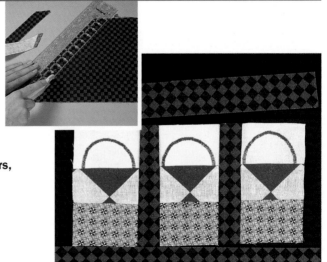

The Quilter's
Problem Solver

Better Drape for Mini Quilts

Problem	Solution
Your tiny quilt is stiff and won't drape nicely on a doll bed.	A gentle hand wash will soften the quilt, especially if it was assembled with unwashed fabrics. Mold the quilt to the bed while slightly damp if necessary, and place it in a well-ventilated area to dry. Next time: Use lawn cotton, which is thinner and lighter than standard quilter's cotton broadcloth. Omit the batting, or try a piece of cotton fabric, possibly flannel, in its place. Used, fabric-softener sheets make a great batting substitute for miniature quilts.

Decorative border stripes are wonderful resources for simulated piecing. They are often made up of coordinating stripes in several widths, all printed side by side along the length of the fabric. Cut parallel to a stripe for ready-made sashing, leaving a ¼-inch seam allowance on each side. Or, jazz up an Attic Windows block by using border stripe fabric to frame each square, rather than plain strips of fabric. Miter the corner seam, matching the stripes for a true framed look.

Try This!

For a quickie finish for your mini quilt, adopt some of these fast and fun ideas:

❏ Finish the quilt with an envelope finish: Place the quilt top and back right sides together, with the optional filler on top, cut to the same size. Stitch around three sides and the corners of the fourth, using a ¼-inch seam allowance. Clip the corners, grade the seam allowances, and turn the quilt right side out. Slipstitch the opening closed.

❏ Use fancy machine stitches to simulate appliqué on a border.

❏ Rubberstamp tiny motifs on plain blocks to simulate handwork in those areas.

Speedy
BIG Quilts

There are times when we need a big quilt in a hurry: to recognize a special person or an upcoming occasion, to support a favorite charity, or to get the bedroom decorating done. Not to worry! Quick needn't mean ordinary, nor large mean labor-intensive. We'll help you make full-, queen-, or king-size quilts that are both fast and fabulous!

Getting Ready

If you're planning to make a bed-size quilt, it helps to know how big to make it. The following measurements give the width and length of standard mattresses:

Bed Size	Mattress Size
Twin	39" × 75"
Full	54" × 75"
Queen	60" × 80"
King	76" × 80"

Add at least 12 inches to each side and to the bottom if you plan to use a dust ruffle. Add at least 18 inches to each side and to the bottom if you prefer to eliminate the dust ruffle and cover both mattress and box spring with the quilt. These measurements assume that you will be using decorative pillows or pillow shams at the head of the bed, so they do not include additional length for a pillow tuck. Add 10 inches to the top of the quilt if you prefer to include a pillow tuck.

What You'll Need

Fabric, prewashed and pressed

Rotary cutter and mat

Acrylic rulers (6" × 24" *and* 12" × 12" or larger square)

Marking pencil

¼" graph paper and colored pencils (or a computer design program)

Calculator (optional)

Pins

Sewing machine

¼" patchwork foot (optional)

Neutral-color thread

Thread snips or embroidery scissors

Iron and ironing board

Big Ideas

Just as it is important to consider scale when making a miniature, **keep proportion in mind as you plan a large-scale quilting project.** A king-size quilt, for example, is probably *not* the project for 6-inch blocks! You'll not only need *lots* of them—defeating the purpose of "speedy"—but also such a small block (with its even smaller pieces) can result in a finished design that is busy or lacks impact.

A good size block for bed quilts is 10 or 12 inches, which provides pleasing visual balance.

Tip

To create good visual balance in *all* components of a large-scale quilt, incorporate hefty widths for sashings, borders, and bindings.

SPEEDY BIG QUILTS

2

Big jobs call for big tools. While it is certainly possible to make large-scale quilts with a standard-issue rotary cutter and a 12-inch ruler, you'll work more efficiently—and more accurately—if you select equipment designed for heavy-duty use. Large (and extra-large) rotary cutters glide through multiple layers, enabling you to save valuable time when cutting. A 24 × 36-inch cutting mat provides an ample surface for cutting more substantial yardages, and a 6 × 24-inch ruler allows you to make longer cuts, eliminating the need to fold and shift fabric continually, two major causes of inaccurate (and slow!) cutting.

Tip

A 12- or 15-inch-square ruler is a handy tool for squaring up large quilt blocks quickly and accurately.

3

For a *super* speedy big quilt, let the fabric be the block! Raid your stash for extra-large florals, landscapes, or novelty prints. Rotary cut them into large squares, 8 inches or larger, and surround them with simple, rotary-cut sashes. Choose wood-look fabrics to simulate frames, or mix and match solids and prints in complementary colors. Tailor the theme to the occasion or recipient: golf or baseball fabrics for a college-bound sports enthusiast, holiday prints for the newly-weds' first Christmas, florals for your gardening mother-in-law.

Tip

Add drama to the "fabric-as-block" quilt by using the Attic Windows pattern. Frame the blocks on two adjacent sides in contrasting fabrics.

4

Log Cabin and Edna's Pinwheel are perfect examples of traditional blocks that are naturals for a quick-pieced big quilt. They are made of rotary-cut strips, pieced by machine with straight seams. Minimal matching is required, and they are both great for using up scraps and extra leftover strips. Keep the finished strip width in reasonable proportion to the size of both the block *and* the overall quilt.

For a speedy Log Cabin, start with a 2½-inch square, then cut 2½-inch-wide strips. Six fabrics surrounding the square will yield a 14-inch block.

Tip

Consider the Rail Fence pattern—another block that lends itself to quick and easy strip piecing.

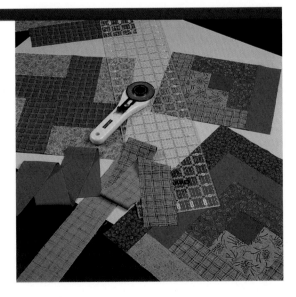

You needn't restrict big quilts to blocks based only on rectangles and squares. **Include blocks with triangles, but stick with those that incorporate straightforward half- and quarter-square triangle units that can be quick-cut and speed-pieced, such as the Double Pinwheel and Ohio Star.**

Review other traditional blocks to see if they adapt well to the speedy big quilt treatment. A good candidate has enough pieces to maintain pleasing proportion when enlarged to 10, 12, or even 15 inches, but not so many that it becomes overly labor-intensive to piece.

Whatever your pattern, never cut an individual square, rectangle, or triangle when you can avoid it! **Instead, examine your overall design carefully for repeating shapes and elements.** Save time by stacking and cutting fabrics into strips, *then* subcutting them into the appropriately sized pieces.

Try a "quickie" method (such as strip piecing or double-stitching triangle squares) to construct ready-made, identical half-square triangle units. See "Once Upon a Triangle Square," starting on page 46, for additional ideas.

Big quilts naturally require more fabric and larger pieces than wall-hangings or lap quilts. With a little planning, you can still work efficiently, with a minimum of fabric waste.

Cut borders, long sashes, and other extra-large pieces (such as setting squares, side and corner triangles) first. **Whenever possible, cut strips that can be subcut for more than one use.** For example, a 3½-inch strip can be subcut into 3½-inch squares *and* 3½ × 6½-inch rectangles.

Tip

Cut the widest strip you need from your fabric first, cut the required patches from it, then recut the strip to the next narrowest width and continue cutting patches.

SPEEDY BIG QUILTS

8

The Crazy Patch makes a fast, fanciful, and fun choice for a large-scale quilt. Its random quality assures that you need not spend time matching points and corners. (And, of course, it provides the perfect opportunity to invade and reduce a growing stash of scraps, remnants, and other oddball pieces.) Start with an irregular four- or five-sided shape, and build each block from the center out, Log Cabin style. You don't necessarily need to work on a foundation; just piece until your block is at least 1 inch larger than your finished size. **Then, trim the block to size using a large square ruler.**

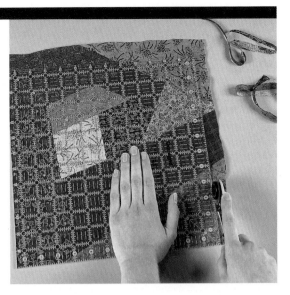

9

Your choice of set can help you to build big quilts even more quickly. For example, alternating plain (unpieced) squares can stretch a limited number of pieced blocks to bed size in no time flat.

A lively, large-scale print makes a good choice for the alternate square in a big quilt. Its visual texture breaks up dead space, while balancing nicely with pieced blocks scaled for a bed. For the quickest and easiest construction, arrange the blocks in straight rows. You won't need to cut setting triangles, piece diagonal rows, or worry where the bias falls.

10

Use rotary-cut sashing strips for another minimum-effort, block-extending setting alternative. Sashing can run vertically or horizontally between rows of pieced blocks for a classic strippy set or both vertically *and* horizontally to create a lattice effect. Whichever you prefer, you'll need fewer blocks.

Stay away from extra-wide lattice sashing; it overwhelms the blocks. Cut sashing no wider than one-fourth the finished measurement of the block (i.e., no wider than 3 inches for a 12-inch block).

Using Up Orphan Blocks

Problem	Solution
You've amassed (or inherited) a collection of mismatched orphan blocks—workshop samples, garage and estate sale finds, plus 30 matching blocks from Aunt Sarah's attic.	Lucky you! You've got the makings of an "instant" big speedy quilt. If the blocks are all the same size, such as Aunt Sarah's Dresden Plates, join them side by side or in any other setting that pleases you: straight, diagonal, sashed, or strippy. If your blocks differ in size, add Log Cabin–style strips to size them identically. Use neutral color fabrics that blend or coordinating colors to keep the quilt from becoming overly busy. Arrange the blocks on a design wall and play with them. Use a Polaroid camera to record arrangements that you like before moving on to something new. Fill in the spaces with your bits and pieces, strips, sashes, oddly sized setting squares, cut-up or partial blocks in varying shapes and measurements. Or piece small checkerboards, strip sets, or Flying Geese units to fit spaces between blocks. Think of it as working on a huge jigsaw puzzle!

Try these quick-finishing techniques on your next quilt—large or small.

❏ **Skip the binding.** Layer the batting, backing (face up), and unquilted top (face down). Sew a ¼-inch seam around the perimeter, leaving an opening large enough to turn the quilt right side out. Tuck in the unfinished seam, and topstitch around the entire edge. Quilt as desired . . . no binding required!

❏ **Leave no mark.** Hand or machine quilt without marking. Quilt around shapes, in the ditch, or an overall pattern.

❏ **Tie it up.** Instead of quilting, tie your quilt with decorative thread, yarn, or ribbon.

Try This!

Chances are, you have strips, squares, rectangles, and triangles left over from previous and in-progress projects. Instead of tossing them into a catch-all scrap bin, sort them by size into large zippered bags or see-through containers. Label the contents by size and shape (3½-inch squares, 2-inch-wide strips, and so on).

You'll be amazed how often projects require similarly sized pieces. Before beginning a new quilt, visit your fabric bank. It can save you *lots* of cutting time—and help you feel virtuous about using up those scraps you've saved for so long!

The Buddy *System*

Double the quilters, double the fun . . . and cut the work time in half! Working with a friend is a great way to share special time while getting the job done. What may seem like repetitive or mundane jobs are suddenly fun when you have company in the sewing room! Once you and your friend finish a quilt or two, you'll never want to quilt alone—you may even want to add a third quilting "buddy" to your get-togethers.

Getting Ready

What You'll Need

Fabrics, prewashed

Rotary cutter, mat, and ruler

Pattern or project directions

Sewing machine

¼" presser foot (optional)

Iron and ironing board

Design wall

Invite a quilting friend to join you for a day of cutting, sewing, pressing, and camaraderie in exchange for a reciprocal arrangement at her house. To take full advantage of the time that you have with a quilting buddy, be sure to have your block or quilt design determined and your fabrics selected and prewashed. Have the cutting directions prepared and at hand. Check to see that you have plenty of thread, and fill several bobbins so that you won't run out during your stitching marathon. Make sure you have enough working area for both quilters. You'll need your usual ample sewing space and a separate space for cutting and/or pressing. If you're used to swiveling from your sewing table in front of you to your pressing/cutting area beside you, you may need to rearrange your space a bit so that your friend has easy access to the space as well and enough room to work without sitting in your lap.

Dividing the Labor

To get the most done in the shortest amount of time, you and your buddy should precut all the strips first. Refer to your block design (a colored, numbered diagram is always a good idea), and cut as many strips as you will need for the number of blocks you plan to make. **One quilter can press the fabric as the other cuts the strips to be used in the blocks.**

Tip

Label each stack of strips so there is no confusion during the sewing phase.

Tip

If the sewer runs out of patches, she can switch to cutting or pressing to help the buddy get ahead.

2

Once all the strips are cut, one quilter can sew while the other makes subcuts and presses. **Chain piecing always makes the process go faster,** and the presser can help make this even speedier by aligning the pieces to be sewn when possible, or handing new pieces to the sewer one at a time. A comfortable rhythm will develop as you work.

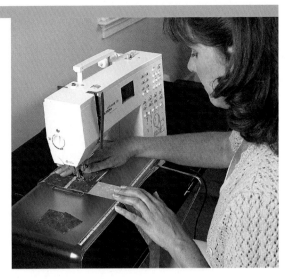

3

When the sewer has a few units chain pieced, the presser can cut the first few units from behind the sewing machine as they emerge from underneath the needle. The presser can trim off any extra fabric or dog ears as necessary to make the units square and ready to join to the next patch.

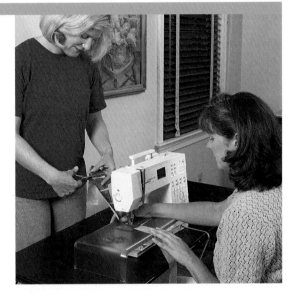

4

The presser can then press the seam allowances on the newly sewn units. With one quilter doing all the pressing (and not being distracted by sewing), it's easier to keep all the seam allowances pressed in the correct direction. After she does a few, she should stack them close to the machine, so they'll be ready for the sewer to pick up, in the correct position for the next step.

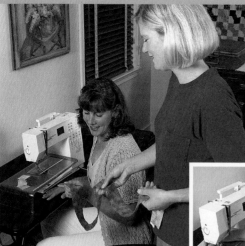

When the sewer finishes all of the first set of units, the presser should have the next patch or strip and the stack of newly pressed units at the ready. The presser can align each pressed unit with the next piece to be sewn, so all the sewer has to do is pick up the pieces and sew. **Again, the sewer will chain piece this new unit,** as the presser snips the units off the chain behind the machine and presses them.

Continue assembling the blocks following the directions and diagram for your project. The presser is responsible for ensuring that each strip is supplied in the correct order and that a stack of pressed units is ready to sew onto the next patch or strip. **All the sewer has to do is pick them up and stitch, but it's a good idea if she double-checks the order.** Buddies are great for catching each other's mistakes!

Tip

Your back and neck can get stiff from long stretches at one task. Take frequent breaks, or trade jobs with your buddy.

Another great advantage of working with a buddy is having a second opinion handy when auditioning the blocks. **Use your design wall to arrange the blocks and decide on a layout.** A second pair of eyes is useful to check for color balance, proportion, and overall visual impact. A buddy can also come up with solutions and creative alternatives that you might never think of.

THE BUDDY SYSTEM

8

Once you know how you want to set the blocks together, the presser can remove the blocks from the design wall two at a time, aligned for sewing together in the correct position. **The sewer can chain piece the blocks together while the presser keeps track of their position in the layout.** If it's a complex layout, the sewer may want to hand the sewn blocks back to the presser to be returned to their position on the design wall after each sewing step.

Tip

Take a Polaroid photo of your layout on the design wall, or sketch it quickly to use as a handy reference.

9

In between handing pairs of blocks to the sewer, **the presser continues her original job, pressing the seam allowances to the side.** Seam allowances should be pressed in opposite directions from row to row so that the seams will butt together when the rows are sewn together.

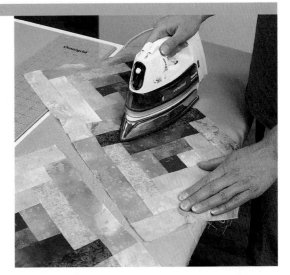

10

When you see how successful and how much fun this method is, you may not want to quilt any other way. If you and your quilting buddy have similar schedules, you'll never have to make a quilt alone again! And just think, you can turn out twice as many quilts in half the time!

The Quilter's
Problem Solver

Correcting Mistakes

Problem	Solution
Stopping to rip out or resew a seam is time-consuming and frustrating.	Assume that you'll make mistakes and plan for them: Begin with two or three extra units, and if you make a mistake when sewing, simply discard that unit and continue on. Best case: You have extra blocks to incorporate into your design or save for another use. Worst case: You waste a little fabric but save the time you would have spent redoing mistakes.
Neither quilter really likes pressing.	Take turns! Make it fun. Plan to switch after a round is completed, or set a timer for a preset amount of time and trade off. Or, invite a third person who likes to press and offer fabric in trade.
Block sizes are inconsistent.	This can happen if more than one person is doing the sewing. Compare seam allowances by having each sewer stitch a sample unit. Be sure that patches are aligned correctly and that each sewer is lining up patches in the machine to obtain an accurate ¼-inch seam. Use a piece of ¼-inch masking tape as a guide if the sewing machine does not have a ¼-inch presser foot. An obvious solution would be for one person to do the piecing throughout a project.

Skill Builder

Quilters who are working quickly are more likely to make mistakes placing fabrics correctly. With a buddy, you have two pairs of eyes looking to prevent these errors before they happen. If you know that one of you is prone to this or other types of "goofs," think ahead and designate a step in your process to double-check the weak point.

Try This!

Have more than one quilting friend? Invite them all and create a real assembly line! Perhaps you can use a larger site, such as the place where your quilt group meets. If you have enough space to spread out, you can have quilters simultaneously precutting patches and strips, sewing units, pressing sewn seams, and crosscutting or squaring up. Or, take turns rotating in and out of the different stations. Bring more than one machine, and have two sewers—whatever fits your project best.

THE BUDDY SYSTEM

Rotary Cutting & Speed Piecing
Glossary

B

Bias edge. On a fabric patch, a cut edge that is at a 45 degree angle to the straight grain of the fabric.

Border print. Fabric with designs or patterns that create decorative stripes of varying widths that run along the lengthwise grain.

C

Chain piecing. Sewing patches, strips, or units together one after the other, without lifting the presser foot or cutting the threads.

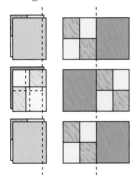

Cheater cloth. Also called faux patchwork or printed patchwork. Printed cloth that mimics a patchwork or appliquéd quilt.

Crosscut. Rotary cutting across a strip set, resulting in units or segments for a block or quilt.

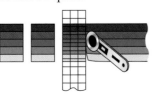

D

Design wall. A vertical surface, usually covered with flannel or batting, on which quilters can experiment with quilt designs and layouts.

Diamond. A shape with four equal sides and opposite angles that are equal. Diamonds are referred to by their acute angles, such as the 45 degree or 30 degree diamond.

Dog ears. Little triangular tabs of fabric that extend beyond the edges of sewn triangle squares.

E

Equilateral triangle. A triangle with 60 degree angles at each corner and three sides of equal length.

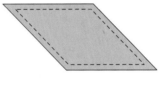

F

Foundation. A layer of material (fabric, paper, interfacing, batting) on which to piece.

Four Patch. A quilt block made up of four square patches, two across and two down.

G

Gradation. A lightening or darkening in the color or value of fabrics that are used side by side in a strip set or quilt.

H

Half-rectangle. A triangle that is made by cutting a rectangle in half diagonally.

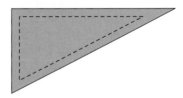

Half-square triangle. A triangle that is made by cutting a square in half diagonally.

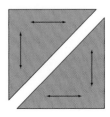

Hexagon. A shape with six equal sides and a 120 degree angle at each corner.

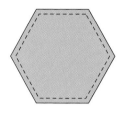

Kite. A shape with two equal and adjacent shorter sides and two equal and adjacent longer sides. Named for the classic child's toy.

Miniature quilt. A small quilt, usually in scale with dolls or dollhouses.

Nine Patch. A quilt block made up of nine squares in a tic-tac-toe configuration: three rows of three.

Octagon. A shape with eight equal sides and a 135 degree angle at each corner.

One Patch. A quilt that contains only one shape patch, repeated over and over, usually with fabrics of varying colors and prints.

Parallelogram. A four-sided shape with opposite sides equal in length and parallel. While squares and rectangles are parallelograms, quilt-makers usually reserve this term for quadrangles with two acute and two obtuse angles.

Quarter-square triangle. A triangle obtained by dividing a square diagonally in half twice, resulting in four triangles each with their longest edges along the straight grain.

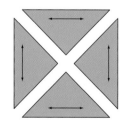

Sashing. Strips of fabric that separate blocks in a quilt. Sashing can be pieced or appliquéd.

Segment. A unit used in quilt-making produced by cutting across the seams of a strip set.

Selvage. The tightly woven edges that run lengthwise along fabric yardage.

Straight grain. Threads that run parallel or perpendicular to the selvages in fabric yardage.

Strip. A narrow piece of fabric. Usually, strips are cut from the crosswise grain (selvage to selvage).

Strip set. Two or more strips of fabric sewn together lengthwise, often cut into smaller units to make portions of a block or quilt.

String piecing. Similar to strip piecing, but usually done on a foundation. Long "strings" of fabric are often irregular in shape and cut from scraps.

Trapezoid. A four-sided shape with two opposite sides parallel. The other two sides are mirror images of each other and at 45 degrees to the long parallel side.

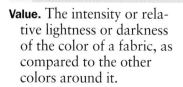

Triangle square. A square made of two right triangles sewn together along their bias edges; also known as half-square triangle, triangle-pieced square, or bias square.

Value. The intensity or relative lightness or darkness of the color of a fabric, as compared to the other colors around it.

Janet Armstrong-Wickell has been quilting for many years, but it became a passion in 1989 when she discovered miniature quilts. She is the sponsor of Minifest, the only national show and seminar devoted to small quilts, and the author of *Quick Little Quilts, The Complete Guide to Making Miniature and Lap Quilts.* For the past few years Janet has been teaching quilting and hand-marbling fabric, and as a freelance writer, she has contributed to many Rodale books.

Barbara J. Eikmeier has been quilting for 15 years and teaching quiltmaking to adults and children for 10 years. She especially loves teaching rotary techniques to beginners and enjoys the moment when her newest students proclaim they are "hooked." She is the author of *Kids Can Quilt* and a coauthor of *Traditional Quilts with Painless Borders.* Barb is married to an Army officer and they currently live in Seoul, South Korea, with their two children. Barb is presently collecting new design ideas influenced by her Asian experiences and the Korean quilters with whom she is becoming acquainted.

Jane Hall and **Dixie Haywood** are award-winning quiltmakers who are known for adapting traditional designs using contemporary techniques and innovative approaches. Their quilts have been exhibited throughout the country and are in private and public collections. Both have been teaching and judging quiltmaking for more than 20 years and have a strong commitment to provide students with well-grounded and creative information so they can make their own unique quilts. They have authored—together and separately—numerous books and magazine articles.

Diane Rode Schneck's first love has always been fabric. Her quilts range from updated versions of classic scrap quilts to original art quilts. Her pieces always include a wide variety of fabrics and frequent touches of humor. Diane's quilts have been exhibited internationally and have appeared in many well-known magazines as well as in several books. She is a cofounder of the popular Phabric Phantom tours, a guided adventure showing quilters and sewers firsthand where to find great fabrics in New York City. Her most popular class, which scrapaholics and packrats especially adore, is called "Scraps, Crumbs, Strings, and Things."

Susan Stein began quilting in 1977 and has been obsessed ever since, enjoying the art in all its facets. She has owned two quilt shops in Minnesota, chaired a national quilt show, served as a state quilt guild president, and taught nationally and locally. She has designed projects for four Singer Sewing Library books and many other publications and has her own published book of designs. Susan especially enjoys making sampler quilts with innovative settings, making Double Wedding Rings with contemporary treatments and embellishments, and using hand-dyed fabrics.

Beth Wheeler has been a freelance designer for 13 years, the last five of which have been devoted to full-time designing and writing in the quilting, sewing, and craft areas. Beth's designs and articles have appeared in a multitude of magazines, books, and special-interest publications. She recently expanded her operations to include a line of craft and quilting patterns and kits. Her art garments and quilts have been in numerous invitational shows and museum exhibits and are in private collections across the country.

Darra Duffy Williamson, author of *Sensational Scrap Quilts,* considers the nineteenth-century scrap quilt one of her greatest sources of inspiration. Her second book will soon be released by the American Quilter's Society. In addition, Darra wrote the popular "Traditional with a Twist" series for *Quilting Today.* In 1989 she was named Quilt Teacher of the Year by *Professional Quilter* magazine and remains much in demand—both in the United States and abroad—for her informative and entertaining lectures and workshops. Her colorful, multifabric quilts are award winners on the local, regional, and national level and are held in private collections throughout the United States and Puerto Rico.

Old Growth by Dixie Haywood

Acknowledgments

Quiltmakers

We would like to thank the following quilt artists who graciously loaned us their original quilts to photograph as examples of the techniques described in this book:

Joanne Adams, Jewel Box, 1998, on page 108

Janet Armstrong-Wickell, Mini quilts, 1999, on pages 102, 104, and 109

Barbara J. Eickmeier, Nine Patch, on page 28

Dixie Haywood, Olé, 1993, on pages 74 and 125, and Old Growth, 1996, on pages 68 and 123

Barbara Reid, The Milky Way quilt, 1999, on page 108, following a pattern from Jean Wells' *Patchwork Quilts Made Easy,* from C&T and Rodale Press (out of print)

Judy Roche, Barn Raising, 1990, on page 10, nineteenth-century basket quilt, 19th century, on page 46, and antique Red & White Birds (1870s) on page 56

Elizabeth Rosenberg, Dog quilt, 1996, on page 62

Diane Rode Schneck, The Fire Inside, 1999, on pages iv and 92, and End of the Day Quilt, 1999, on page 95; both copyright Diane Rode Schneck

Karen Soltys, Lone Star, 1991, on page 32

Susan Stein, Woven in Red, 1996, on pages ii and 42, and Hunter's Star, 1999, on page 80

Beth Wheeler, Hollyhocks, 1999, on page 86

Sample Makers

The following quilters made samples for this book:

Janet Armstrong-Wickell, Sarah S. Dunn, Barbara J. Eikmeier, Jane Hall, Dixie Haywood, Eleanor Levie, Diane Rode Schneck, Karen Soltys, Susan Stein, and Beth Wheeler

Fabrics and Supplies

We also thank the following companies for contributing equipment and materials for use in the photography:

Alaska Dyeworks—fabrics

Benartex, Inc.—fabrics

Bernina of America, Inc.—Virtuosa 150 sewing machine

Clotilde—thread racks

Cranston Print Works Company—fabrics

Robert Kaufman Co.—fabrics

Olfa/O'Lipfa—rotary cutters and blades

Omnigrid, Inc.—rulers and cutting mats

Rose & Hubble—fabrics

Rowenta—DE-92 Professional iron

Wright's/EZ International—Tri-Recs tools

Alaska Dyeworks
300 W. Swanson
Suite 106
Wasilla, AK 99654
(907) 373-6562
Web site: www.akdye.com
E-mail: akdye@akdye,com
Gradated fabric bundles in light to dark, blends, marbled

Sonya Lee Barrington
837 47th Avenue
San Francisco, CA 94121
(415) 221-6510
Bundles of of hand-dyed, gradated fabrics

Cherrywood Fabrics
P.O. Box 486
Brainerd, MN 56401
(218) 829-0967
¼-, ½-, and 1-yard bundles of gradated fabrics in light to dark, blends, and mixtures, plus yardage; send $8 for swatch card

Clotilde, Inc.
B3000
Louisiana, MO 63353
(800) 772-2891
www.clothilde.com
Thread racks, rotary cutter blade guards, sewing notions

Come Quilt with Me
3903 Avenue I
Brooklyn, NY 11210
(718) 377-3652
Brooklyn Revolver, quilter's acrylic templates

Fiskars, Inc.
7811 West Stewart Avenue
Wausau, WI 54401
(715) 849-4011
www.fiskars.com
Rotary cutters, scissors

Keepsake Quilting
Route 25B
P.O. Box 1618
Centre Harbor, NH 03226
(800) 865-9458
(800-TO-KWILT)
Fax: (603) 253-8346
Mat smoother

LP Sharp
HC3, Box 48 A
Emily, MN 56447
Rotary blades resharpened; include SASE for return

MeasureMatic, Inc.
995 West K Street
Benicia, CA 94510
(707) 745-1138
Miracle Ironing Board Cover

Omnigrid, Inc.
P.O. Box 663
1560 Port Drive
Burlington, WA 98233
(800) 755-3530
Rulers and mats

Primrose Gradations
P.O. Box 6
Two Harbors, MN 55616
(218) 252-0619 or
(888) 393-2787
Web site: www.dyearts.com
Bundles of gradated fabric in light to dark, blends, and mixtures, plus yardage

Shades, Inc.
585 Cobb Parkway S
Nunn Complex Studio O
Marietta, GA 30062
(800) 783-3933
Web site:
shadesText@aol.com
Variegated fabrics in light to dark

Wright's
85 South Street
P.O. Box 398
West Warren, MA 01092
(800) 628-9362
Web site: www.wrights.com
Tri-Recs tools

Olé by Dixie Haywood

Index

H

Half-rectangles
    assembling pairs of, 64–65
    cutting, 22–23, 65, 67
    designing with, 63–64,
      66–67
    pressing, 66–67
Half-square triangles, 57–61,
    106. *See also* Triangle
    squares
Hanging techniques, 15
Hexagons, cutting, 24
Hunter's Star block, 81–82

I

Indian Trails block, 53
Irish Chain block, 34–35

J

Jack-in-the-Box block, 50
Jacob's Ladder block, 53, 100

K

Kaleidoscope block, 38
Kitchens, as workspace, 13
Kite shapes, cutting, 27

L

Lady of the Lake block, 52
Landscape quilts, 66–67
Lattice. *See also* Sashing
    gradated, 45
    half-rectangles in, 66–67
    for miniature quilts,
      106.
Light boxes, 76
Log Cabin block, 110
Lone Star block, 37

M

Marking, eliminating, 113
Mattress sizes, 109
Measurements, cutting and, 19
Miniature quilts
    checkerboard for, 106
    finishing, 107
    prints for, 103–4
    sashing for, 104, 106
    stiffness in, 107
    stripes for, 104–7
Mistakes
    correcting, 119
    in foundation piecing, 72
    preventing, 119

N

New York Beauty block, 75–76

Nine Patch block
    constructing, 28–31
    miniature, 105
    strip piecing, 34
    triangle squares in,
      49–50
Notions, storing, 15

O

Octagons, cutting, 25
Ohio Star block, 111

P

Parallelograms, cutting, 26
Parent strips, defined, 21
Paths and Stiles block, 36
Pinwheel block
    for bed quilts, 110
    half-rectangles in, 67
    triangle squares in, 51
Plaids, grain of, 58
Pressing
    accurate cutting and, 17
    in buddy system, 116–19
    half-rectangles, 66–67
    seam allowances, 66–67,
      118
    triangle squares, 48
Prints, for miniature quilts,
    103–4
Pyramid block, 21

Q

Quilts
    bed-size, 108–113
    hanging, 15
    miniature, 102–7

R

Rail Fence block
    for bed quilts, 110
    miniature, 104
    strip-pieced, 35–36
Rectangles. *See also* Half-rec-
    tangles
    cutting, 22–23
    strip piecing, 36–37
Ripping out, 119
Rotary cutters
    caring for, 17
    for large quilts, 110
    sharpening, 41
    tips for using, 8–9
Rulers
    for large quilts, 110
    slippage of, 19, 67
    storing, 17

as templates, 38
variations in, 8, 19

S

Safety, tips for, 8–9
Sashing
    for bed quilts, 112
    foundation-pieced, 77
    for miniature quilts, 104
    strip-pieced, 39–40
Sawtooth borders, 54
Scraps
    crazy piecing with, 78
    from diamonds, 24
    from Rail Fence block, 35
    storing, 113
    string piecing with, 92–95
    for triangle squares, 61
Seam allowances
    on foundations, 70, 73
    pressing, 66–67, 118
Settings
    half-rectangles, 63
    triangle squares, 53–54
Slippage, when cutting, 19, 67
Snail's Trail block, 84–85
Spider Web block, 38
Squares, strip-pieced, 37. *See
    also* Triangle squares
Stabilizers
    for curves, 75–77
    for sashing, 77
Stitch in the ditch, faux, 103
Stitch length, for foundation
    piecing, 71, 79, 82
Stretch prevention, in founda-
    tion piecing, 71, 79
String piecing
    blocks, 94–95
    fabrics for, 93
    foundations for, 93
    miniature, 105
Stripes
    grain of, 58
    as strip sets, 104–7
Strip piecing
    bindings, 41
    block patterns, 34–36
    borders, 40
    color gradations, 38,
      42–45
    corner squares, 39–40
    sashing, 39–40
    shapes, 36–38
    stripes as, 104–6
    techniques for, 33
    yardage, 86–91

INDEX

INDEX

METRIC EQUIVALENCY CHART

mm=millimeters
cm=centimeters

Yards to Meters

YARDS	METERS	YARDS	METERS	YARDS	METERS	YARDS	METERS	YARDS	METERS
1/8	0.11	21/8	1.94	41/8	3.77	61/8	5.60	81/8	7.43
1/4	0.23	21/4	2.06	41/4	3.89	61/4	5.72	81/4	7.54
3/8	0.34	23/8	2.17	43/8	4.00	63/8	5.83	83/8	7.66
1/2	0.46	21/2	2.29	41/2	4.11	61/2	5.94	81/2	7.77
5/8	0.57	25/8	2.40	45/8	4.23	65/8	6.06	85/8	7.89
3/4	0.69	23/4	2.51	43/4	4.34	63/4	6.17	83/4	8.00
7/8	0.80	27/8	2.63	47/8	4.46	67/8	6.29	87/8	8.12
1	0.91	3	2.74	5	4.57	7	6.40	9	8.23
11/8	1.03	31/8	2.86	51/8	4.69	71/8	6.52	91/8	8.34
11/4	1.14	31/4	2.97	51/4	4.80	71/4	6.63	91/4	8.46
13/8	1.26	33/8	3.09	53/8	4.91	73/8	6.74	93/8	8.57
11/2	1.37	31/2	3.20	51/2	5.03	71/2	6.86	91/2	8.69
15/8	1.49	35/8	3.31	55/8	5.14	75/8	6.97	95/8	8.80
13/4	1.60	33/4	3.43	53/4	5.26	73/4	7.09	93/4	8.92
17/8	1.71	37/8	3.54	57/8	5.37	77/8	7.20	97/8	9.03
2	1.83	4	3.66	6	5.49	8	7.32	10	9.14

Inches to Millimeters and Centimeters

INCHES	MM	CM	INCHES	CM	INCHES	CM
1/8	3	0.3	9	22.9	30	76.2
1/4	6	0.6	10	25.4	31	78.7
3/8	10	1.0	11	27.9	32	81.3
1/2	13	1.3	12	30.5	33	83.8
5/8	16	1.6	13	33.0	34	86.4
3/4	19	1.9	14	35.6	35	88.9
7/8	22	2.2	15	38.1	36	91.4
1	25	2.5	16	40.6	37	94.0
11/4	32	3.2	17	43.2	38	96.5
11/2	38	3.8	18	45.7	39	99.1
13/4	44	4.4	19	48.3	40	101.6
2	51	5.1	20	50.8	41	104.1
21/2	64	6.4	21	53.3	42	106.7
3	76	7.6	22	55.9	43	109.2
31/2	89	8.9	23	58.4	44	111.8
4	102	10.2	24	61.0	45	114.3
41/2	114	11.4	25	63.5	46	116.8
5	127	12.7	26	66.0	47	119.4
6	152	15.2	27	68.6	48	121.9
7	178	17.8	28	71.1	49	124.5
8	203	20.3	29	73.7	50	127.0